Richard Harding Davis

The Cuban and Porto Rican Campaigns

Richard Harding Davis

The Cuban and Porto Rican Campaigns

ISBN/EAN: 9783337378370

Printed in Europe, USA, Canada, Australia, Japan

Cover: Foto ©Andreas Hilbeck / pixelio.de

More available books at **www.hansebooks.com**

THE CUBAN AND PORTO RICAN CAMPAIGNS

BY

RICHARD HARDING DAVIS, F.R.G.S.

AUTHOR OF "SOLDIERS OF FORTUNE," "GALLEGHER AND OTHER STORIES," "THE PRINCESS ALINE," ETC.

ILLUSTRATED

NEW YORK
CHARLES SCRIBNER'S SONS
1898

CONTENTS

CHAPTER I.
THE FIRST SHOT . . . . . .   PAGE 1

CHAPTER II.
THE FIRST BOMBARDMENT . . . 24

CHAPTER III.
THE ROCKING-CHAIR PERIOD 45

CHAPTER IV.
THE VOYAGE OF THE TRANSPORTS 86

CHAPTER V.
THE GUASIMAS FIGHT 120

CHAPTER VI.
THE BATTLE OF SAN JUAN 173

CHAPTER VII.
IN THE RIFLE-PITS 224

CHAPTER VIII.
THE PORTO RICAN CAMPAIGN 296

LIST OF ILLUSTRATIONS

	PAGE
OFFICERS WATCHING THE ARTILLERY PLAY ON COAMO . *Frontispiece*	
KEY WEST HOTEL	2
THE FIRST PRIZE OF THE WAR, *BUENA VENTURA*, SHOWING SOME OF THE PRIZE CREW ON HER DECK	9
GROUP OF PRIZES—KEY WEST	13
THE FLAG-SHIP *NEW YORK* CLEARED FOR ACTION	16
"MESSENGER!"	18
THE FIRST PRISONER OF THE WAR	20
THE FLAG-SHIP *NEW YORK* UNDER WAY AT FULL SPEED IN CUBAN WATERS	25
THE ADMIRAL'S BRIDGE	28
LIEUTENANT MULLIGAN AND ENSIGN BOONE	29
JUNIOR OFFICERS OF THE *NEW YORK*	32
SUNDAY INSPECTION ON BOARD THE *NEW YORK*	38
LOBBY—TAMPA BAY HOTEL	47
TAMPA BAY HOTEL PIAZZA	49
CORRESPONDENT BARGAINING FOR A HORSE	52
A GROUP OF WAR CORRESPONDENTS	54
MAJOR-GENERAL JOSEPH WHEELER	55
CAPTAIN ARTHUR H. LEE AND COUNT VON GOETZEN, BRITISH AND GERMAN MILITARY ATTACHÉS	57
FOREIGN ATTACHÉS AT TAMPA	59
GENERAL VIEW OF THE CAMP AT TAMPA, EIGHTH INFANTRY IN THE FOREGROUND	61
FIRST ARTILLERY HORSES BATHING IN THE SURF	64
LEAVING THE WATER	65

LIST OF ILLUSTRATIONS

	PAGE
SECOND INFANTRY DRILL AT TAMPA	67
AN ARTILLERY BRIGADE	77
THIRD CAVALRY AT DRILL	81
"WHO SAID OATS?"	84
PORT TAMPA ON DAY OF SAILING OF TRANSPORTS	87
GENERALS MILES AND SHAFTER ON DECK OF THE TRANSPORT *SEGURANÇA* AT PORT TAMPA	91
ARTILLERY FOR CUBA	93
WAITING FOR THE EXPEDITION TO MOVE	95
GENERAL MILES ON THE DAY OF SAILING OF TRANSPORTS	97
TRANSPORTS OFF FOR CUBA	99
GENERAL SHAFTER AT PORT TAMPA SUPERINTENDING EMBARKATION	101
ADMIRAL SAMPSON AND GENERAL SHAFTER GOING ASHORE AT ASERRADEROS	104
CAPTAIN STEWART BRICE BEING CARRIED ASHORE AT ASERRADEROS	106
GENERALS SHAFTER AND GARCIA WITH CUBAN VOLUNTEERS	109
A CHEER BY THE ROUGH RIDERS	118
COLONEL ROOSEVELT	121
COLONEL ROOSEVELT AND RICHARD HARDING DAVIS	122
LANDING OF AMERICAN FORCES AT SIBONEY	124
ANOTHER VIEW OF THE LANDING	126
A GROUP OF OFFICERS	129
CAPTAIN O'NEILL OF THE ROUGH RIDERS	134
AMERICAN BOATS LANDING CUBANS AT SIBONEY	138
THE PLACE WHERE THE GUASIMAS FIGHT BEGAN	143
SIBONEY, FROM THE HILL OVER WHICH THE WOUNDED ROUGH RIDERS RETIRED AFTER THE FIGHT	147
A GROUP OF ROUGH RIDERS	152
WOUNDED ROUGH RIDERS COMING OVER THE HILL AT SIBONEY	157
MAP OF THE COUNTRY BEFORE SAN JUAN	174
GENERAL CHAFFEE IN THE FIELD	176

LIST OF ILLUSTRATIONS

	PAGE
The Farm House Below El Poso Hill	179
Stone Breastwork with Palm-leaf Roof at South Side of El Caney	181
Men of the Twelfth Infantry on the Firing Line at El Caney	184
Brigadier-General Sumner and Aides	187
The War Balloon Making its First Ascension	189
Capron's Battery in Action at El Caney	191
Gun No. 1 of Grimes's Battery	195
Artillery Coming up El Poso Hill	197
El Poso, Immediately After the Spanish Fire Ceased	200
Grimes's Battery at El Poso	201
Fording a Stream on the Way to the Front	205
Mule Train Carrying Ammunition from Siboney to San Juan	207
General Hospital of the First Division	210
The Fight at the San Juan Block-house, July 1st	215
San Juan Block-house, Showing Marks of Shot	219
The San Juan Hill, Showing General Wheeler's Camp	221
United States Troops in the Trenches before Santiago	225
Making Observations while Under Heavy Spanish Fire	228
Looking Toward Santiago from the Trenches of the Colored Troops	233
A Detachment of the Seventy-first New York Volunteers just Before Going into Action	239
Digging Trenches Before Santiago, about July 10, 1898	242
Generals Wheeler, Chaffee, and Lawton in Consultation	243
Outside Trenches of the Second Infantry	245
Trench to Right of San Juan Block-house Occupied by American Troops	249
The Trenches of the Fourth Infantry	253
Looking to the Left Down the Trench of the Second Infantry	257
Looking Toward Santiago from the Trenches in Front of the San Juan Block-house	259

LIST OF ILLUSTRATIONS

	PAGE
THE SPANISH PRISONERS BEING ESCORTED TO THE LINES TO BE EXCHANGED FOR HOBSON AND HIS *MERRIMAC* CREW	263
ANOTHER VIEW OF THE SPANISH PRISONERS ON THE WAY TO BE EXCHANGED	267
BLINDFOLDED SPANISH PRISONERS ON THE WAY TO THE MEETING-PLACE BETWEEN THE LINES	271
ARTILLERY ENTRENCHED	274
HOBSON'S *MERRIMAC* CREW ARRIVING WITHIN THE AMERICAN LINES, JUST AFTER THE EXCHANGE	275
SAN JUAN BLOCK-HOUSE—AMERICAN TROOPS IN TRENCHES	279
TRENCHES OF THE FIRST CAVALRY BEFORE SANTIAGO	284
LIEUTENANT WILLIAM TIFFANY	287
RAISING THE FLAG OVER SANTIAGO	289
THE TRENCHES OF THE ROUGH RIDERS ON SAN JUAN HILL	293
JOHN FOX, JR., WAR CORRESPONDENT	295
SEAL OF THE CORPORATION OF THE CITY OF PONCE	296
THE *GLOUCESTER* BOMBARDING JUANICA, PORTO RICO	297
GENERAL MILES IN LAUNCH OF *MASSACHUSETTS* TOWING PONTOONS, AT JUANICA, PORTO RICO	301
CAPTAIN HENRY H. WHITNEY	304
UNITED STATES ARTILLERY ENTERING PONCE	307
MAP SHOWING LOCATION OF UNITED STATES MILITARY TELEGRAPH LINES AND OFFICES	311
ENSIGN CURTIN OF THE *WASP*	312
TROOPS ENTERING PONCE	313
GENERAL MILES AND STAFF IN THE PATIO OF THE HOTEL FRANÇAIS AT PONCE	315
MARKET PLACE AT PONCE	317
CROSSING THE RIVER RIO BUCANA	320
AMERICAN SOLDIER SHOWING A RIFLE TO SPANIARDS	321
UNLOADING ARMY SUPPLIES FROM THE TRANSPORTS AT PORT PONCE	323
CITY TROOPS MARCHING THROUGH THE TOWN OF SANTA ISABEL	327
ARREST OF A SPANISH SPY IN PONCE	330

LIST OF ILLUSTRATIONS

	PAGE
CITY TROOP ON ROAD BETWEEN GUAYANA AND PONCE	332
GENERAL WILSON ENTERING COAMO	333
CITY TROOP MARCHING ON ROAD BETWEEN PONCE AND GUAYANA	335
THIRD WISCONSIN ENTERING COAMO	337
THE WOMEN OF COAMO RECEIVING THE AMERICAN SOLDIERS	339
COLONEL BIDDLE, OF GENERAL WILSON'S STAFF, INTERROGATING A SPANISH PRISONER	342
THIRD WISCONSIN VOLUNTEERS PASSING SPANISH RIFLE-PIT THROWN UP ACROSS THE STREET IN COAMO	345
MAIN ROAD BETWEEN PONCE AND PORT PONCE	348
MAP OF THE SPANISH POSITION NEAR AIBONITO	349
OFFICERS OF FIRST CITY TROOP OF PHILADELPHIA	351
BATTERY "A," UNDER CAPTAIN WARBURTON, LOADING LIGHTER WITH GUNS	356
TROOPS EMBARKING FOR HOME	357
SENTRIES AT CAVALRY OUTPOST ON CAYEY ROAD, ABOUT TWO AND A HALF MILES FROM GUAYANA	359

MAPS

SANTIAGO DE CUBA AND VICINITY	160
GENERAL MAP OF CUBA	*End of volume*
GENERAL MAP OF PORTO RICO	" "

THE CUBAN AND PORTO RICAN CAMPAIGNS

CHAPTER I

THE FIRST SHOT

IT was half-past four on the afternoon of April 22d, and that peace which only exists when the sun is at 103° brooded over the coral islands of Key West and over the war-ships of the North Atlantic Squadron in her bay. The flags at the mast-heads moved irritably in the hot air, the palms at the Custom-house moved not at all, but were cut against the glaring blue sky like giant petals of tin; in the streets the colored drivers slept in their open hacks, and on the porch of the hotel a row of officers in white duck and of correspondents in yachting-caps sat with tilted chairs and with their feet on the railings before them, in a state of depressed and sweltering silence.

For two months they had been waiting at Key

THE CUBAN AND PORTO RICAN CAMPAIGNS

West. They had waited while the President's message had been postponed once, and three times while Representatives and Senators moved and amended and referred, while foreign powers had offered services more or less friendly, and while

Key West Hotel.

all the machinery of diplomacy had been put in motion to avert or to delay the inevitable end. And they had lost hope and interest. For three weeks the White Squadron had been disguised in a war-paint of lead. The decks of the war-ships had been cleared for action, and the great battleships that were to lead the way, and which stood seven miles nearer to the goal than the others, for three weeks had strained and tugged at their anchorage, like dogs struggling in their chains.

Ever since February the 15th, when the *Maine* settled into the mud of Havana Harbor, these men at Key West had held but one desire and one hope, and at half-past four of that hot and peaceful afternoon their reward came. It wore, when it came, the obvious and commonplace garb of every day. A small boy fell off his bicycle in front of the hotel and ran his eyes along the porch until they rested on a correspondent of the New York *Herald*. To him he handed a telegram, and, mounting his wheel again, rode away up the hot and dusty street. The correspondent opened the envelope with his thumb, and read: "Rain and hail," and started; and then, seeing that the watchful eyes of half the row were upon him, turned his back and took a narrow code-book from his pocket, and ran his finger down its page. He held it toward me, as I stood looking over his shoulder, and I read: "Rain and hail"—"War is declared, fleet ordered to sea." A few moments later the porch was empty, the hall of the hotel was piled high with hand-bags and sailors' kits, and hackmen were lashing their horses down the dusty street; and at the water's edge one could see launches, gigs, and cutters streaking the blue surface of the bay with flashes of white and brass; signal flags of brilliant reds and yellows were spreading and fluttering at the signal halyards; wig-waggers beat the air from the bridges, and across the water, from the decks of the monitors, came the voices of the men answering the roll: "One, two, three, FOUR! *one, two, three,* FOUR!"

There were still ships to coal, or Captain Sampson, who had become Admiral Sampson since half-past four, would on the word have started to blockade Havana. But as they could not be left behind, all of those ships that were ready were moved outside the harbor and the fleet was signalled to be in readiness to start at four o'clock the next morning. That night as the sun sank—and it sinks at Key West with a splendor and glory that it assumes in but few other ports in the world—it spread a fiery red background for thirteen black ships of war outlined with gallows-like yards against the sky. Some still lay at anchor, sparkling with cargo lights and with the coaling barges looming bulkily along side, and others moved across the crimson curtain looking less like ships than a procession of grotesque monsters of the sea—grim, inscrutable, and menacing.

THE FIRST SHOT

War had been declared. It had come at last, and, as the fleet lay waiting for the day, it is a question if any man in the squadron slept that night, but did not instead keep watch alone, and wonder what war might bring to him. To whom would it bring honor, to whom honor with death, to whom would the chance come, and who would seize it when it came, and who would make it come?

In the quick changes of war and under its cruel tests, unknown men would become leaders of men, and those who had attained high places and had risen and fattened in the days of peace would be pushed aside into oblivion; the political generals would see a gunner's mate become in an hour the nation's hero; new conditions and new problems would rise, to find men ready to grasp them. Anything was possible—new alliances, new enemies, and new friends. The declaration of war meant all these things—a new map and a new chapter in the history of the world.

And yet while men wondered as to what the morrow might bring forth, the physical aspect of the night was one in strange contrast to the great change of the day. We could imagine the interest and excitement which the declaration of war had roused in all corners of the country; we knew that for the moment Key West was the storm-centre of the map of the United States, and that where the squadron would go, what it would do, and how soon it would move upon the enemy were questions that men were asking in clubs and on street corners; we knew that bulletin-boards were blocking the streets of lower New York with people eager for news, and that men and women from Seattle to Boston were awake with anxiety and unrest.

And yet at the heart of it all, in the harbor of Key West, save for the water lapping against the great sides of the ships and the bells sounding in chorus across the stretches of the bay, there was only silence, and the night wore every aspect of peace. For though all through that night the vessels talked with one another, they spoke in a language of signs—a language that made less sound than a whisper. That was the only promise for the morrow, their rows of lanterns winking red and white against the night, and vanishing instantly in mid-air, and the great fingers of the search-lights sweeping grandly across the sky, halting upright for a moment, and then sinking to the water's edge, measuring out the heavens and carrying messages of command to men many miles at sea.

THE FIRST SHOT

The morning of the 23d awoke radiantly beautiful with light and color. In the hollows of the waves deep blue and purple shadows caught the million flashes of the sun, and their white crests danced in its light. Across this flashing picture of light and movement and color, the leaden-painted war-ships moved heavily in two great columns, the battle-ships and monitors leading on the left, the cruisers moving abreast to starboard, while in their wake and on either flank the torpedo-boats rolled and tossed like porpoises at play. To the active imagination it might have appeared that each was racing to be the first to throw a shell into Cabáñas prison, to knock the first stone from the ramparts of Morro Castle, to fire the first shot of the War of '98. But the first shot of the war was reserved for no such serious purpose.

For while the houses of Key West were still well in view, there came into the lines of the squadron a courteous Spaniard, who, unsuspecting and innocent of war, steered his tramp steamer, the *Buena Ventura*, into the very jaws of the enemy. And it was upon him that the unsought-for honor fell of receiving the first shot our navy had fired " in anger " in thirty years.

According to the story of the Spanish captain,

as told that same afternoon in the harbor of Key West, when he saw so many "beautiful" war-ships flying the American flag, he said to himself: "Behold! the courtesy of my race requires that I salute these beautiful war-ships." Those are his exact words. And in admiration and innocence the poor man raised the red and yellow standard of Spain.

This was at half-past five in the morning of April 23d. Lieutenant Frank Marble was officer of the deck on the flag-ship, and from the forward bridge he had reported the presence of a vessel on the starboard bow. The admiral signalled the ship nearest the *Buena Ventura*, which happened to be the *Nashville*, "What colors does the stranger show?"

Both the *Helena* and the *Nashville* signalled back "Spanish," and the answer came from the flag-ship to the *Nashville*, "Capture her."

The signal as it is in the code-book is really much fuller than that, but that is its meaning. So the *Nashville* fired a shot across the *Buena Ventura's* bow. Patrick Walton fired it. It was the first shot of the war. A second shot followed, and the *Buena Ventura* hove to, and a prize crew, under Ensign Magruder, boarded her; and a press-boat buried her bows in the water

The First Prize of the War, *Buena Ventura*, Showing Some of the Prize Crew on her Deck.

THE FIRST SHOT

and rushed back to the United States with the news that the squadron had taken her first prize, and that the blockade had begun. And so it came about that a fluttering of flags and a couple of shots aimed at a flashing, dancing sea formed the first hostile act of our war with Spain.

For twelve days after war was declared the flag-ship *New York* lay ten miles off Morro Castle, blistering in the sun by day and made beautiful by the moon at night. She was the central office of the blockading squadron, and from her messenger-boys, in the shape of black and grimy torpedo-boats, carried orders to the men-of-war that stretched along the coast from Cardenas to Bahia Honda. While they lay waiting or patrolling their stations, alert and watchful, the flag-ship planned and arranged and issued commands. She was the bureau of information for the fleet, the mouth-piece of the Strategic Board at Washington, and all through the hot brilliant days her red and yellow signals fluttered and flapped and her wig-waggers beat the air. Other war-ships drew up beside her, and their officers came on board to receive instructions; tug-boats converted into auxiliaries flew to her for aid, to ask for the loan of a few casks of drinking-water, or the services of a mechanic to mend a leak, or to deliver the mail-bags and, what was of equal value, clothes from the laundry.

The *New York* was the clearing-house of the fleet, the first to receive the news, the one place from which news was disseminated. It came to us from officers of prize-crews on their way back to their ships, who halted to report to the Admiral and to tell their adventures to the ward-room mess; and it was brought to us by the fleet of press-boats, which in return received the news of the day on the flag-ship. Sometimes they received this through a megaphone, sometimes they sent a correspondent over the side to get it at first hand, and sometimes, when the sea was rough, we threw it to them done up in a glass bottle. The flag-ship was the only place from which to view and comprehend the blockade. What was seen from a press-boat was at long range; from its deck the motive and result of any move was of necessity problematical. It was like reporting the burning of the Waldorf-Astoria from the Brooklyn Bridge. The observer in the distance might see much smoke and some flame, but whether the cause of the fire were accidental or incendiary, whether there were loss of life or deeds of heroism, he could only guess.

In its creature-comforts life on board the flag-

Group of Prizes—Key West.

ship was like that on board of a yacht cruising in summer seas; but overshadowing its comforts was an organization as complete as that of the Bank of England, and discipline as absolute as that of a monastery. In no military post, from Knightsbridge Barracks to Gibraltar, from Fort Houston to Fort Sill, nor in Greece, Egypt, France, Russia, or Germany have I seen discipline better observed, or such "smartness," or such intelligent obedience as I noted during the ten days that I remained on the *New York*. In that time there were many novel experiences to impress one; there was much that was entirely new and quite incomprehensible. There were some exciting races after blockade-runners, some heavy firing, some wonderful effects of land and sea and sky, some instances of coolness and courage and of kindness and courtesy; but what was more impressive than all else besides, was the discipline of the ship's company and the perfection of her organization. Many men can swagger and be brave and shoot off a gun. That our sailors are brave no one has ever doubted, even before the victory of Manila Harbor; but the best sailor is the man who not only can stand by his gun, but who can stand watch eight hours on end without stealing a few minutes' sleep; who respects himself, his ship, and her officers; who is as thoroughly in earnest when he is alone cleaning a bit of brasswork as when he is aiming a four-inch gun in the presence of the enemy.

The discipline of the *New York* was rigid, intelligent, and unremitting, and each of the five

The Flag-ship *New York* Cleared for Action.

hundred men on this floating monastery moved in his little groove with the perfect mechanism of one of the eight-inch guns. A modern war-ship is the perfection of organization. It is the embodiment of the axiom that "a stitch in time saves nine." It is the eternal vigilance which obtains on board that keeps her what she is, the hourly fight against rust and dust that makes her always look as though she had just been made complete that morning. All the old homely sayings seem to be the mottoes of her executive. There is "a place for everything and everything in its place," whether it is a projectile weighing half a ton, or signal flag No. 22, or a roll of lint for the surgeon, or the blue-jacket in charge of the search-light.

A ship of war is like a moving village. She has to house and feed and give employment to her inhabitants, and to place them at certain points at a moment's notice, to face unknown conditions and to face them coolly and intelligently. You can imagine the confusion in a village of five hundred people should they be dragged out of bed at midnight by an alarm of fire. But in the floating village of the war-ship *New York* discipline and training have taught the inhabitants to move to certain places, and to perform certain work when they get there, within a space of two minutes. It is so on every other war-ship in the Navy of the United States. And it does not consist entirely in manning a gun and pulling a lanyard. That is the showy work—the work that tells in the despatches, and which is illustrated in the weekly papers.

There are also those who serve "who only stand and wait"; who see nothing of the fighting, but take equal risk with those who fight; who are not inspired by the consciousness that all is going well, but who remain at their posts in the semi-darkness below decks, shaken by concussions above, and not knowing how soon the sides of the ship may part, or the decks below rise, or a projectile crash bursting and burning through the deck above and choke them with vile suffocating fumes. They feed the fires with coal and haul on ammunition-lifts, like miners in a coal-pit. Their work is just as important as is that of the gunner who trains and fires the big gun; but when it is over they go back to set the table for the officers' mess, or to play a bass viol in a string band, or sweep out the engine-rooms. They are just as valuable to the village as is the gunner's mate, and they should be remembered.

"Messenger!"

THE FIRST SHOT

Admiral Schley remembered them at the time of the destruction of Cervera's fleet, and every few minutes sent messengers below decks to the engine-rooms to tell the men there how the fight was going, and that the American ships were driving the Spanish vessels from the sea. They were deserving of such consideration; for a more earnest, alert, and self-respecting class of men than are on our war-ships are not to be found in any class or profession in our country, and that is as true of the admiral as of the crew, and of the crew as of the admiral.

It was very difficult to believe that we were really at war. A peaceful blockade does not lend itself to that illusion. From the deck of the *New York*, we overlooked the coast of Cuba as from the roof of a high building; and all that we saw of war was a peaceful panorama of mountain-ranges and yellow villages, royal palms and tiny forts, like section-houses along the line of a railroad, and in the distance Morro Castle and the besieged city of Havana basking in a haze of glaring sunlight.

So, the first prisoner of the war was almost as much of a surprise to the ship as the ship was to him. Up to the time of his arrival a Spaniard, to most of the officers and crew, was an unknown quantity—a picture of a bull-fighter in the comic papers, something hidden away somewhere along the smiling line of coast. The first prisoner introduced us to the enemy, and his uniform of blue drill, his Panama hat, and his red and yellow cockade made the Spaniard for the first time

The First Prisoner of the War. The Spaniard is the one pulling his mustache; Sylvester Scovel is in the centre, in a yachting suit and cap.

real and human. I had seen Spanish officers in Cuba swaggering in cafés and plazas, tramping at the head of their troops through dusty roads, directing the burning of huts and cane-fields, and giving the order to fire on insurgent prisoners, and I must confess to a sneaking sense of joy when this poor Second Lieutenant came silently into Captain Chadwick's cabin twisting his hat between his hands, and sank gratefully into the chair they placed for him. The first question Captain Chadwick asked was whether he would have breakfast, but the prisoner said he had no appetite; then the captain offered him a cigar, but he shrugged his shoulders and bowed and said he did not care to smoke. Then the Captain told Sylvester Scovel, who was interpreting, to ask the prisoner to say from where he came, and how he happened to get caught. But to every one of these questions Scovel added six of his own, inquiring as to how many troops the Spaniards had placed along the coast, where forts were situated, where patrols met, and how deep the water was in certain ports. Every now and then Chadwick would say, "That will do, tell him he is free;" but Scovel would object: "No, don't let him go yet; he is telling me things he shouldn't."

And then Scovel would smile with innocent blue eyes upon the prisoner, and nod encouragingly, and the unhappy Lieutenant would proceed to give him the information which the blockading squadron desired.

The name of Sylvester Scovel is probably better known in Cuba than that of any other

American, even than that of Fitzhugh Lee. He is certainly more cordially hated than any other of the "nation of pigs," and a reward of $10,000 was for some time placed upon his head. The Spaniards captured him once, after he had eluded them hundreds of times; the Senate of the United States demanded that he should be set at liberty, and after a month's imprisonment he was released. If he had been taken in Cuba during the war, he would have been shot or hung on the instant; and the death of no other hanged American would, I believe, have caused such universal rejoicing among Spanish officers and Spanish residents. Consequently, it was rather amusing to see the Spanish Lieutenant, Juan de Rio, clinging close to Scovel's elbow, and showing him the utmost deference and gratitude. Scovel wore a yachting cap and a suit of blue serge, so it is probable that the Spaniard mistook him for one of the ship's junior officers. But when they parted, after Scovel had shown him over the ship, there was a little scene. They had said farewell with many flourishes, and the Spaniard had, after the fashion of his race, made a pretty speech to the effect that he saw it was impossible to surpass the courtesy of an American officer as to surpass his war-ship.

THE FIRST SHOT

"You have been most kind to me," he added, "and I should like to know your name. I shall always remember it."

Scovel laughed and nodded. "My name is Sylvester Scovel," he said, bowing. "I am the correspondent of the New York *World*."

The Spanish have no sense of humor, and this one could not rise to the occasion. He only gasped and stared, and backed hastily away. He can hardly be blamed. It must be bewildering to find that you have been overwhelmed with courtesies by the man whose death, had he been your prisoner and you had killed him, would have brought you a reward of $10,000 and a vote of thanks from your Government.

CHAPTER II

THE FIRST BOMBARDMENT

WHILE I was on board the *New York* the big guns were twice brought into service—once at the bombardment of the batteries at Matanzas, and again when they were trained on some impudent cavalry men who had fired on the ship from the shore. Why they did so, unless they had heard that French cavalry once captured a fleet of war-ships, it is impossible to say. The first of these bombardments was chiefly important because it was the first; the second was of no importance at all.

The quarter of an hour during which the firing lasted at Matanzas was of interest in giving some knowledge of how a war-ship in action acts upon herself. With land forces the effect of their fire upon the enemy is the only thought; on the sea, in one of these new inventions of warfare, the effect of the batteries on the ship herself is an added consideration.

The bombardment of the shore batteries at

The Flag-ship *New York* Under Way at Full Speed in Cuban Waters.

Matanzas came out of a clear sky. We knew something unusual was going forward, but only that. We had been lying off Morro and suddenly started at good speed to the east, and when we reached Matanzas we came slowly in toward the mouth of the harbor and then drifted. The *New York* was nearly two miles away from the shore, but with a glass one could see soldiers gathered on a long rampart of fresh earth. To the naked eye the yellow soil made a line against the green manigua bushes on the point.

I was in a gun-turret on the main deck listening to a group of jackies disagreeing as to whether the port before us was that of Matanzas or Cardenas. I had visited both places and ventured the opinion that it was Matanzas. So they crowded in to ask about the houses that we saw on shore, and as to whether there were mines in the harbor, and what we were doing there anyway; and I was just congratulating myself on having such a large and eager audience, when someone blew a bugle and my audience vanished, and six other young men came panting into the gun-turret, each with his hair flying and his eyes and mouth wide open with excitement.

I asked if that particular bugle call was "general quarters," and a panting blue-jacket as he rushed by shouted "Yes, sir!", over his shoulder and ran on. Everybody was running—officers,

The Admiral's Bridge.

middies, and crew. Everyone seemed to have been caught just at the wrong end of the ship and on the wrong deck, at the exact point farthest from his division. They all ran for about a minute in every direction, and then there was absolute silence, just as though someone had waved a wand over each of them and had fixed him in his place. But it was apparently the right place. Captain Chadwick ran down the ladder from the forward bridge, and shouted at Ensign Boone, "Aim for 4,000 yards, at that bank of earth on the point." Then he ran up to the bridge again, where Admiral Sampson was pacing up and down, looking more like a calm and scholarly professor of mathematics than an admiral. For the Admiral is a slow-speaking, quiet-voiced man, who studies intently and thoughtfully the eyes of everyone who addresses him; a man who would meet success or defeat with the same absolute quietness; an intellectual fighter, a man who impresses you as one who would fight and win entirely with his head.

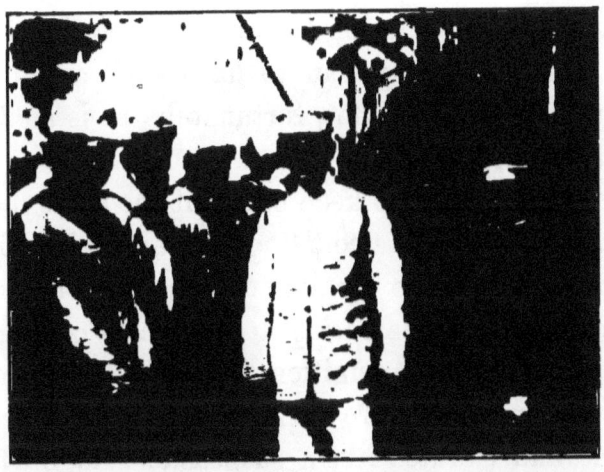

Lieutenant Mulligan in the Centre. Ensign Boone, who Fired the First Shot at Matanzas, is on the Right.

Ensign Boone's gun was in the waist amidships, and he had been especially chosen to fire the first gun because the Captain had picked him out from among the other junior officers as an eager and intelligent ensign, and also because the jealousy that rages between the eight-inch guns in the fore and after turrets is so great that not even the Admiral himself would dare to let one of them fire the first shot of the war—that is, the first shot "with intent to kill"—for fear of hurting the feelings of the others. So Captain Chadwick cut the knot by ordering Ensign Boone to let loose first. It was a proud moment in the life of Ensign Boone, and, as he is one of the class that was turned out of Annapolis before its time, he is a very young man to have such an honor thrust upon him. But, fortunately, he is modest and bore it bravely.

At first I tried to keep count of the shots fired, but soon it was like counting falling bricks. The guns seemed to be ripping out the steel sides of the ship, and to be racing to see which could get rid of the most ammunition first. The thick deck of the superstructure jumped with the concussions, and vibrated like a suspension-bridge when an express train thunders across it. They came crashing from every point, and, when you had steadied yourself against one volley, you were shaken and swayed by the backward rush of the wind from another. The reports seemed to crack the air as though it were a dense body. It opened and shut and rocked you about with invisible waves. Your ear-drums tingled and strained and seemed to crack. The noise was physical, like a blow from a base-ball bat; the noise itself stung and shook you. The concussions were things apart; they shook you after a fashion of their own, jumping your field-glasses between the bridge of your nose and the brim of your hat and hammering your eyebrows. With this there were great clouds of hot smoke that swept across the decks and hung for a moment, hiding everything in a curtain of choking fog, which had a taste of salt, and which rasped your throat and nostrils and burned your eyes.

The ship seemed to work and to fight by herself; you heard no human voice of command, only the grieved tones of Lieutenant Mulligan, rising from his smoke-choked deck below, where he could not see to aim his six-inch gun, and from where he begged Lieutenant Marble again and again to "Take your damned smoke out of my way." Lieutenant Marble was vaulting in and out of his forward turret like a squirrel in a cage. One instant you would see him far out on the deck, where shattered pieces of glass and wood-work eddied like leaves in a hurricane, and the next pushing the turret with his shoulder as though he meant to shove it overboard; and then he would wave his hand to his crew inside and

Junior Officers of the *New York*. Ensign Boone in the Centre.

there would be a racking roar, a parting of air and sea and sky, a flash of flame vomiting black smoke, and he would be swallowed up in it like a wicked fairy in a pantomime. And instantly from the depths below, like the voice of a lost soul, would rise the protesting shriek of Dick Mulligan asking, frantically, " Oh, WILL you take your damned smoke out of my way ! "

The *New York* did not have all the fighting to herself, for the *Puritan* and the *Cincinnati* were a few hundred yards out at sea, and almost broke their signal halyards in begging the Admiral to be allowed to come in too. They were like school-boys snapping their fingers at the schoolmaster in their eagerness to show off their knowledge, and well they showed it. An impudent battery had opened from the eastern coast of the harbor, and they turned on that. The *Puritan* was a wonderful sight. Her decks were lashed with two feet of water, the waves seemed to be running in and out of her turrets, and the flames and smoke from her great guns came from the water-line, so that it looked to us as though she were sinking and firing as she sank. The *Cincinnati* fired broadsides as rapidly as a man can shoot a self-cocking revolver; it was perhaps the most remarkable performance of the day. The aim throughout was excellent—although it is not necessary to say that of American marksmanship —and the shots fell fairly in the ramparts, throwing the earthworks fifty feet in the air and cutting them level with the ground. Only three shots from the batteries struck near the *New York*, and none of them came closer than one hundred yards. The engagement lasted fifteen minutes, but it was so exciting while it lasted that they did not seem more than five.

On the whole, the concussions were not as deafening as I had been led to think they would be, but what the effect would be on one, if an enemy's shots of like force were striking and bursting around the ship, I cannot even imagine. The thought of it makes me want to take off my hat to every blue-jacket I meet.

No shots passed near us, but I found the wear and tear from our own guns alone during that quarter of an hour in which they were in action far more trying than all the Turkish shells had been at Velostinos, when they raced continuously overhead for the better part of two long, hot days. But there you were a free agent; you only moved because you thought you were going to be hit. On the *New York* you moved because you could not help yourself, because the guns of your own side beat you about and deafened and blinded and shook you.

It is not likely that anyone will undervalue the qualities of our sailors, but no one need feel the least afraid of giving them too much honor, or of praising them beyond their deserts. Their footing on one of these floating iron-foundries in action is about as secure as that of a parcel of flies on a window-pane when someone hits it with a rock. With the army, a soldier always has the satisfaction of knowing that, if he is not victorious, he can retreat through several States before he is forced into the Pacific Ocean, but the sailor of our navy has no such consolation. He must either win, or sink in his coffin.

One night, just at the dinner-hour, the flag-ship passed the harbor of Cabáñas, which opens in the land a few miles west of Mariel. As she skirted in near shore there was a rattle of volley firing to the left. It appeared to come from a group of buildings on a hill that at one time formed a part of the *centrale* of the Count de la Runion, who owns the sugar plantation of La Herradura, or the Horseshoe, as it is called on account of the way the land curves around the fresh water lake which lies east of Cabáñas Harbor.

The firing continued for some minutes, but it sounded so futile, so inadequate, and so impertinent that those on the deck of the flag-ship gazed shoreward in astonishment, and no one moved to reply.

It grew louder and bolder, and an officer said: "That should be answered;" but as he spoke a stoker leaning out of the hatch of the *Porter*, grimy and sweating and black, took his pipe from between his teeth and laughed.

We could hear his laugh across the water. It was sublime in its irony. It was perhaps the best answer that anyone could have made; but volley firing could not be taken only as a joke, and so the four-inch guns in the stern were run out and turned on the Horseshoe.

It was as ill-chosen a name for that building under the circumstances, as was *Buena Ventura* for that first prize of the war.

The four-inch gun was aimed at the Horseshoe and struck the roof, and as it spoke the deck of the flag-ship heaved as suddenly as an elevator starts when it rises with a jerk, and for a few moments the gun continued to hurl flashes of flame and clouds of hot smoke and volleys, that shook the leaves of the palms and echoed among the hills of Cuba.

It was just at sunset, when the sky was blazing with a gridiron of red and gold. On the decks and on the superstructure, in the turrets and on the bridges, the blue-jackets and the marines crowded together, leaning forward and

THE FIRST BOMBARDMENT

peering into the fading light. As each shell struck home they whispered and chuckled as though they were seated in the gallery at a play, for there had been no general call to quarters. It was only a bit of gun practice in passing, intended to teach infantrymen not to interfere with their betters, and possibly also to discover if there were any masked batteries near Cabáñas which might be tempted by the bombardment to disclose their hiding-places. Meanwhile from below came the strains of the string band playing for the officers' mess, and the music of Scheur's "Dream of Spring" mingled with the belching of the four-inch gun.

This is not a touch of fiction, but the reporting of cold coincidence, for war as it is conducted at this end of the century is civilized.

The ship ran up nearer to the shore, and as she did so a troop of cavalry galloped into view across the fields and formed a cordon under a great tree. What evil purpose they intended toward the *New York* a mile out at sea did not disclose itself, for Captain Chadwick, who was below decks, chose to aim the last shot himself. He trained the four-inch gun on the group around the tree and pulled the lanyard.

There was the same flash as before; it lit up

the faces of the officers and crew as though they were being taken in a flash-light photograph. There was the same backward rush of pungent smoke, the same bellowing roar, and the same upheaval of the massive deck, but when the smoke had cleared there was no cavalry troop

Sunday Inspection on Board the *New York*.

around the tree. The horsemen were riding madly in fifty directions, like men at polo, and at a speed unequalled even in their retreats before machete charges.

But I still think the answer of the grimy stoker was the better one.

We had several calls to "general quarters" at night. They were probably the most picturesque moments of the ten days spent on the flag-ship. To the landsman one bugle-call was like another; "general quarters" meant no more to him than the bugle-call which announced that the mail was going ashore in ten minutes. It was three sleepy Japanese stewards who told me we were going into action. Whenever I woke to find them in the wardroom, I knew someone was going to fire off a six-inch gun.

They opened a hatch just beyond my berth and pulled on a creaking ammunition-hoist. They did this drowsily and stiffly, with the clutches of sleep still on their limbs, and heavy on their eyelids. The officers would run by buttoning tunics over pajamas, and buckling on swords and field-glasses. Even below decks you could hear the great rush of water at the bows and the thumping of the engines, which told that the ship was at racing speed; and when you had stumbled on deck the wind sweeping past awoke you to the fact that in two minutes five hundred men had fallen out of hammocks and into cutlasses and revolvers, and that the ship was tearing through the dark water in pursuit of a bunch of lights. There were no orders shouted, but wherever you peered in the darkness—for the flag-ship showed no lights—you discerned silent, motionless figures.

They were everywhere—on the bridges, at the foot of the gangways, grouped around the guns, crouched in the turrets. You tumbled over them at every step; you saw them outlined against the stars.

And then, shining suddenly from the flying bridge and rising and reaching out across the waves, would shoot the finger of the search-light. It showed the empty waters, and the tossing white-caps in a path of light. "To the left!" a voice would call from the height of the forward bridge, and, as though it were a part of the voice, the light shifted. "No, higher!" the voice would call again, and the obedient light would rise, turning the glare of day upon a half-mile more of troubled water and exposing on its horizon a white, frightened steamer, scudding at full speed for her life. Sometimes she backed, sometimes she changed her course, but the light never loosened its clasp. It gripped her like a thief held in the circle of a policeman's lantern.

It was like a cat playing with a mouse, or a hound holding a fox by its scent. In the silence of the great war-ship, where the darkness was so great that the men, crowded shoulder to shoulder, could not see each other's face, the blockade-runner, exposed and pointed out and held up to our derision, seemed the only living thing on the surface of the waters. She was as conspicuous as a picture thrown by a stereopticon on a screen. And then one of the forward guns would speak, flashing in the night like a rocket and lighting up the line of the deck and the faces of the men, and it would speak again and again. And the flying steamer, helpless in the long-reaching clutch of the search-light, and hearing the shells whistle across her bows, would give up the race and come to a standstill, sullen and silent.

While I was on the *New York* I received a cablegram asking me to relate how the crew behaved during the action at Matanzas. I did not answer it, because I thought there were a few things the American people were willing to take for granted, and because the bombardment at Matanzas was no test of the courage of the crew, but of its marksmanship. There is a story, however, which illustrates the spirit of the men on the *New York*, and which answers, I think, any queries that anyone may make as to how they might behave in action.

Taylor, a young gunner's mate, was shot on April 26th by a revolver. It was an accident; but it is possible he was more seriously hurt than was any of the six wounded men who went through the seven hours' battle at Manila, for the ball passed through his arm and into his right side, and came out nearly a foot away under his left armpit. Junior Surgeon Spear said that, if he had tried to dodge the vital parts in Taylor's body with a surgical instrument, he could not have done it as skilfully as did the bullet, which was neither aimed nor guided by a human hand. It was Junior Surgeon Spear who performed the operation, while the Fleet Surgeon, Dr. Gravatt, watched him and advised. It was a wonderful operation. It lasted nearly two hours, and it left the layman uncertain as to whether he should the more admire the human body or the way a surgeon masters it. What they did to Taylor I cannot tell in technical language, but I know they cut him open and lifted out his stomach and put it back again and sewed him up twice. He could not get wholly under the influence of the ether, and he raved and muttered, and struggled so that at times it required the efforts of two men to hold him down. Just before the Surgeon began to operate the boy gave the Chaplain his mother's address, and reached out his hand and said, "So long, Chaplain."

He was a typical New York boy. He came

from Brooklyn, but nevertheless he looked and talked and thought as you would expect and hope that an apprentice from the *St. Mary's* training-ship would look and talk and think. His skin was as tough as a shoe which had remained long in the salt water, but it was beautifully white and spotless, like a girl's, and the contrast it made with the skin which the sun and wind had tanned was as sharp as the stripes on the flag.

When the second part of him was sewn up Taylor was carried to a cot. He lay there so still that I thought he was dead, and, as it was, they had to inject strychnine into his veins to keep his heart beating. But a minute later he opened his eyes and turned them to the operating-table, where he remembered in a half-drunken way they had placed him two hours before. His eyes were dazed with the ether, his lips were blue, and his face was a ghastly gray. He looked up at the four figures leaning over him, their bare arms covered with his blood, and back at the operating-table that dripped with it. What had happened, who had attacked him, and why, he could not comprehend. He did not know that parts of him which had lain covered for many years had been taken out and held up naked, palpitating, and bleeding to the ruthless light of the sun, to the gaze of curious messmates crowded at the end of the sick-bay; that these parts of himself had been picked over and handled as a man runs his fingers over the keys of a piano, and had then been pushed and wedged back into place and covered over as one would sew a patch on an old sail, to lie hidden away again for many, many years more.

He only knew that some outrageous thing had been done to him—that he had been in a nightmare in hell; and to Taylor, still drunk with ether, these men whose wonderful surgery had saved his life were only the bloody assassins who had attempted it and failed.

He was pitiably weak from loss of much blood, from the shock of the heavy bullet that had dug its way through his body, from the waves of nausea that swept over him, but the boy opened his eyes and regarded the surgeons scornfully. Then he shook his head from side to side on the pillow and smiled up at them.

"Ah, you'se can't kill me," he whispered. "I'm a New Yorker, by God! You'se can't kill me."

That is the spirit of the men who sunk the Spanish fleet at Manila and at Santiago, and of the crew of the war-ship that is named after the city of New York.

CHAPTER III

THE ROCKING-CHAIR PERIOD

AFTER Dewey's victory on May 1st, and while Sampson was chasing the will-of-the-wisp squadron of Spain, the army lay waiting at Tampa and marked time. The army had no wish to mark time, but it had no choice.

It could not risk going down to the sea in ships as long as there was the grim chance that the Spanish fleet would suddenly appear above the horizon line and send the transports to the bottom of the Florida Straits. The army longed to be "up and at them." It was impatient, hot, and exasperated; but there was true common-sense in waiting and a possible failure in an advance without a convoy, and so it continued through the month of May to chafe and fret and perspire at Tampa. Tampa was the port selected by the Government as the one best suited for the embarkation to Cuba. There is a Port of Tampa, and a city nine miles inland of the same name. The army was distributed at the port and in the pine woods back of the city; and the commanding generals of the invading army, with their several staffs, made their head-quarters at the Tampa Bay Hotel.

And so for a month the life of the army was the life of an hotel; and all those persons who were directly or indirectly associated with the army, and who were coming from or going to Key West, halted at this hotel and added to its interest. It was fortunate that the hotel was out of all proportion in every way to the size and wealth of Tampa, and to the number of transient visitors that reasonably might be expected to visit that city. One of the cavalry generals said: "Only God knows why Plant built an hotel here; but thank God he did."

The hotel stands on grounds reclaimed from the heavy sand of the city. It is the real oasis in the real desert—a giant affair of ornamental brick and silver minarets in a city chiefly composed of derelict wooden houses drifting in an ocean of sand; a dreary city, where the sand has swept the paint from the houses, and where sand swamps the sidewalks and creeps into the doors and windows. It is a city where one walks ankle-deep in sand, and where the names of avenues are given to barren spaces of scrubby under-

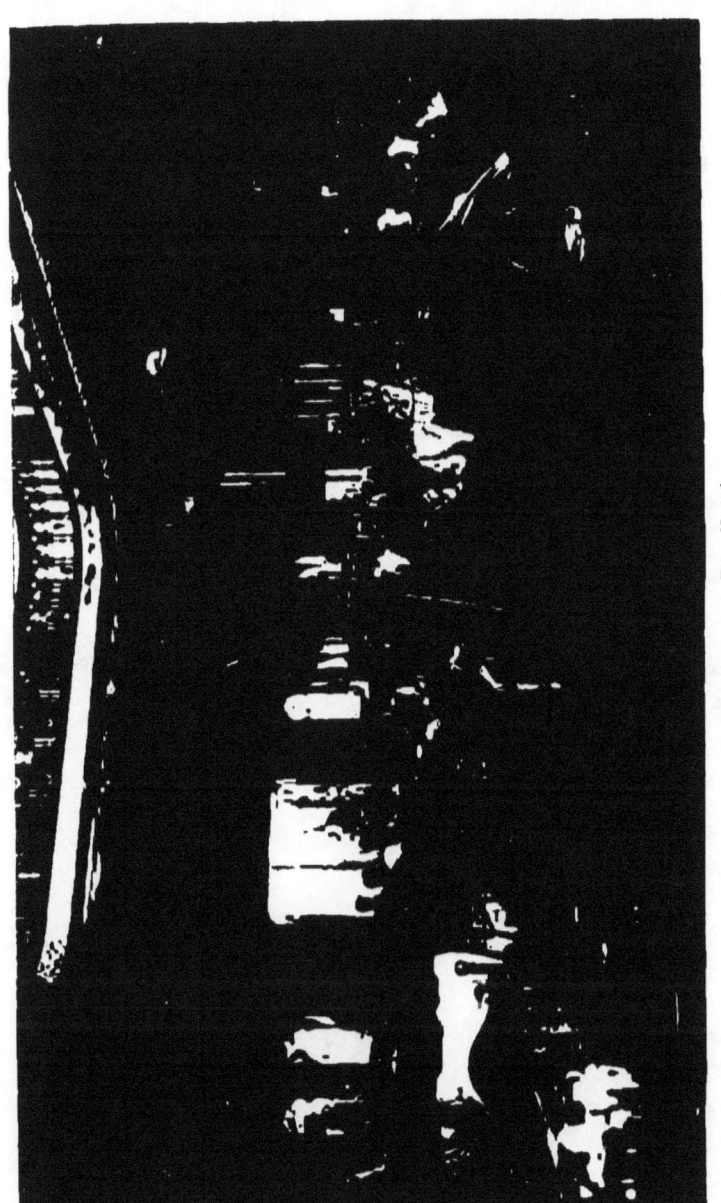

Lobby – Tampa Bay Hotel.

growth and palmettoes and pines hung with funereal moss.

In the midst of this desolation is the hotel. It is larger than the palaces which Ismail Pasha built overnight at Cairo, and outwardly not unlike them in appearance, and so enormous that

Tampa Bay Hotel Piazza.

the walk from the rotunda to the dining-room helps one to an appetite.

Someone said it was like a Turkish harem with the occupants left out. For at first there were no women at the hotel. It was an Eveless Eden, and during the early part of May the myriads of rocking-chairs on the long porches were filled with men. This was the rocking-chair period of the war. It was an army of occupation, but it occupied the piazza of a big hotel.

Everyone believed that the army was going to move in two days. "Well, certainly by Monday," they would say. So at first everyone lived on a war basis. All impedimenta were shipped North. White linen was superseded by flannel shirts, collars were abandoned for polka-dot kerchiefs. Men, fearing the mails would prove too slow, telegraphed for supplies, not knowing that they could walk North and back again before the army would move.

Those were the best days of the time of waiting. Officers who had not met in years, men who had been classmates at West Point, men who had fought together and against each other in the last war, who had parted at army posts all over the West, who had been with Miles after Geronimo, with Forsythe at Wounded Knee, with Hardie and Hunter in the Garcia campaign along the Rio Grande, were gathered together apparently for an instant onslaught on a common enemy, and were left to dangle and dawdle under electric lights and silver minarets. Their talk was only of an immediate advance. It was to be "as soon as Sampson smashes the Cape Verde

THE ROCKING-CHAIR PERIOD

fleet." " It will be all over in two weeks," they said. " We're not going to have a look in at all," they growled. " Do you know what we are? We're an army of occupation, that's all we are. Spain will surrender when her fleet is smashed, and we'll only march in and occupy Havana." So they talked and argued and rocked and drank gallons of iced tea, and the hot days wore into weeks. Life then centred around the bulletin-board; men stood eight deep, peering over each other's shoulders as each new telegram followed fast and was pasted up below the last. Outside, in the sun, horse-dealers from every part of the State led their ponies up and down before the more or less knowing eyes of dough-boy officers and war correspondents; and this daily sale of horses was the chief sign of our activity—this and the frequent reappointment of commanding generals.

One day General Wade was the man of the hour, the next it was General Shafter; and every day came promises of the arrival of the Commander-in-Chief himself. " Miles is coming in a special car," everybody told everybody else. " Now we shall certainly start," everybody said; and each man began to mobilize his laundry, and recklessly paid his hotel bill, and went over his campaign kit for the thirtieth time. But the Commander-in-Chief did not come until after many false alarms, and gloom fell upon the hotel; and many decided it would be cheaper to buy it outright

Correspondent Bargaining for a Horse.

than to live there any longer, so they slept under canvas with the soldiers, and others shaved again and discarded piece by piece the panoply of war. Leggings and canvas shooting-coats gave way to white duck, fierce sombreros to innocent straw hats; and at last wives and daughters arrived on the scene of our inactivity, and men unstrapped their trunks and appeared in evening dress. It was the beginning of the end. We knew then that whether Sampson smashed the ubiquitous fleet or not, we were condemned to the life of a sea-side summer resort and to the excitement of the piazzas. The men who gathered on those piazzas were drawn from every part of the country and from every part of the world, and we listened to many strange stories of strange lands from the men best fitted to tell them. Lieutenant Rowan, just back from six weeks with Garcia, and bronzed and hidden in an old panama hat, told us of the insurgent camp; Major Grover Flint, who had been "marching with Gomez," told us of him; William Astor Chanler, in the uniform of a Cuban colonel, from which rank he was later promoted to that of captain in our own Volunteer Army, talked of Africa with Count von Goetzen, the German military *attaché*, who was also an African explorer; Stephen Bonsal and Caspar Whitney, both but just back from Siam, discoursed on sacred elephants and white ants; and E. F. Knight, the London *Times* correspondent, lingered with the army of the rocking-chairs for a day before swimming into Matanzas Harbor and going to Cabañas prison. Captain Dorst tried to explain why the *Gussie* expedition failed, as though its name were not reason enough; and young Archibald, who accompanied it, and who

Frederic Remington.   Caspar Whitney.   Richard Harding Davis.
                      Grover Flint.   Capt. Arthur H. Lee, R.A.,
                                        British Military *Attaché*.

A Group of War Correspondents.

was the first correspondent to get shot, brought wounds into contempt by refusing to wear his in a bloody bandage, and instead hid his honors under his coat.

There were also General O. O. Howard and Ira Sankey, who busied about in the heat, preaching and singing to the soldiers; Miss Clara Barton, of her own unofficial Red Cross Army; Mr. George Kennan and Mr. Poultney Bigelow, who had views to exchange on Russia and why they left it, and General Fitzhugh Lee, looking like a genial Santa Claus, with a glad smile and glad greeting for everyone, even at the risk of his becoming Vice-President in consequence; and there was also General "Joe" Wheeler, the best type of the courteous Southern gentleman, the sort of whom Page tells us in his novels, on whom politics had left no mark, who was courteous because he could not help being so, who stood up

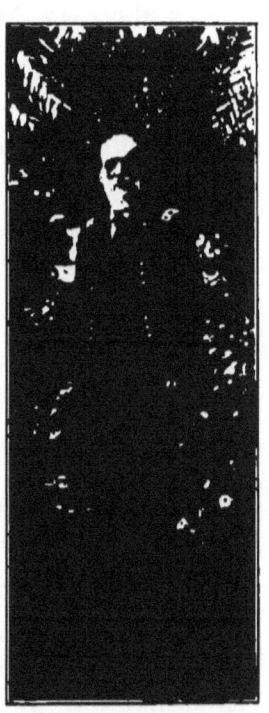

Major-General Joseph Wheeler.

when a second lieutenant was introduced to him, and who ran as lightly as a boy to help a woman move a chair, or to assist her to step from a carriage. There was also, at the last, Lieutenant-Colonel Theodore Roosevelt, with energy and brains and enthusiasm enough to inspire a whole regiment; and there were military *attachés* in strange, grand uniforms, which kept the volunteer army gaping.

But the two men of greatest interest to the army of the rocking-chairs were probably America's representative, Frederic Remington, and Great Britain's representative with our army, Captain Arthur H. Lee. These two held impromptu receptions at every hour of the day, and every man in the army either knew them or wanted to know them. Remington was, of course, an old story; but Lee, the new friend and the actual sign of the new alliance, ran him close in popularity. There was no one, from the generals to the enlisted men, who did not like Lee. I know many Englishmen, but I know very few who could have won the peaceful victory this young captain of artillery won; who would have known so well just what to see and to praise —and when to keep his eyes and mouth shut. No other Englishman certainly could have told

American stories as well as he did and not have missed the point.

Many strange experiences and many adventures

Captain Arthur H. Lee and Count von Goetzen, British and German Military *Attachés*.

had fallen to the lot of some of these men; and had the war been delayed a little longer, the stories they told under the colored lights of the broad verandas would have served for a second "Thousand and One Nights," and would have held as great an interest. They were as familiar with the Kremlin as with the Mosque of St. Sophia, with Kettner's Restaurant as with the Walls of Silence. They knew the love-story of every consul along the Malaysian Peninsula and the east coast of Africa, and why he had left home; they disagreed as to whether laced leggings or heavy boots are better in a Borneo jungle; they talked variously in marks, taels, annas, and shillings; they had been chased by elephants and had shot rhinoceri; and they had themselves been fired over, with the Marquis Yamagata in Corea, with Kitchener in Egypt, with Maceo in Cuba, and with Edhem Pasha in Thessaly. One of them had taken six hundred men straight across Africa, from coast to coast; another had explored it for a year and a half without meeting a white man. This man had explored China disguised as a Chinaman and Russia as a Russian; that had travelled more hundreds of miles on snow-shoes than any other American, Indian, or Canadian. There was one who had been to school with an emperor, and another who had seen an empress beheaded, and Captain Paget, the English naval *attaché*, who had shot thirteen lions, and then, feeling some doubt as to his nerve, dropped four thousand feet out of a balloon to test it.

On the whole, it was an interesting collection

Foreign *Attachés* at Tampa.

of men—these generals with new shoulder-straps on old tunics, these war correspondents and military *attachés*, who had last met in the Soudan and Greece, and these self-important and gloomy

Cuban generals, credulous and mysterious; these wealthy young men from the Knickerbocker Club, disguised in canvas uniforms and Cuban flags, who are not to be confused with the same club's proud contribution to the Rough Riders. There were also women of the Red Cross Army, women of the Salvation Army, and pretty Cuban refugees from Havana, who had taken a vow not to dance until Havana fell. Each night all of these people gathered in the big rotunda while a band from one of the regiments played inside, or else they danced in the big ball-room. One imaginative young officer compared it to the ball at Brussels on the night before Waterloo; another, less imaginative, with a long iced drink at his elbow and a cigar between his teeth, gazed at the colored electric lights, the palm-trees, the whirling figures in the ball-room, and remarked sententiously: "Gentlemen, as General Sherman truly said, ' war is hell.' "

Four miles outside of this hotel, sleeping under the pines and in three inches of dirty sand, there were at first ten thousand and then twenty-five thousand men. They were the Regulars and Volunteers, and of the two the Volunteers were probably the more interesting. They were an unknown proposition; they held the enthusiasm

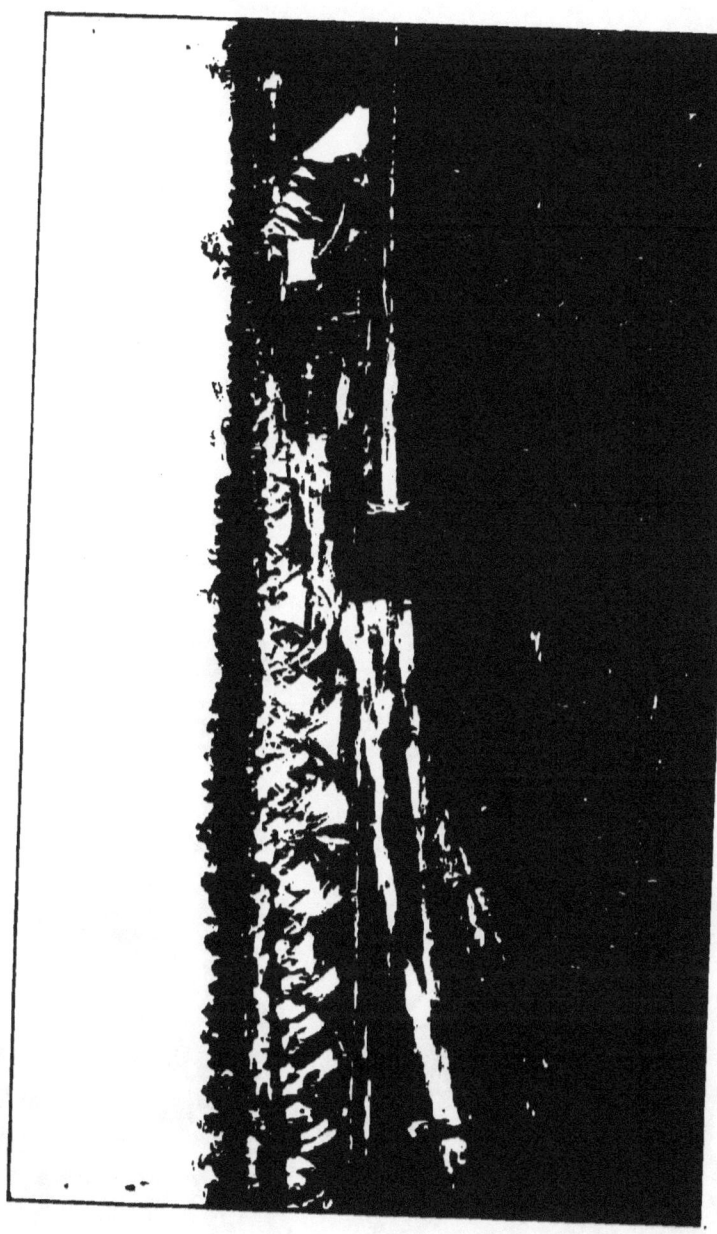

General View of the Camp at Tampa. Eighth Infantry in the Foreground.

of amateurs; they were making unusual sacrifices, and they were breaking home-ties which the Regulars had broken so long before the war came that the ties had had time to reknit. The wife or mother of the Regular had grown accustomed to his absence, and had arranged her living expenses on a basis of his monthly pay; the family of the Volunteer, on the contrary, was used to see him come home every evening and hang his hat in the hall, and had been living on the salary he received as a book-keeper, salesman, or mill-hand. So the Volunteers had cares for those at home which the Regulars did not feel, as well as the discomforts of the present moment. Neither of them showed much anxiety as to the future.

The first two regiments of Volunteers to arrive at Lakeland, which lies an hour's ride farther back than Tampa, were the Seventy-first New York and the Second Massachusetts. They made an interesting contrast. The New York men were city-bred; they had the cockney's puzzled contempt for the country. Palm-trees, moss hanging from trees, and alligators were as interesting to them as the first sight of a Pathan prisoner to a British Tommy. Their nerves had been edged by the incessant jangle of cable-cars and the rush and strain of elevated trains. Their palates had been fed on Sunday papers and Wall Street tickers; their joys were those of the roof-gardens, and Muschenheim's, of Coney Island, and

First Artillery Horses Bathing in the Surf.

the polo grounds. The Massachusetts men, on the other hand, were from the small towns in the western half of Massachusetts; they were farmers' sons, and salesmen in village stores; some of them were country lawyers, and many of them worked in the mills. They took to the trees and lakes contentedly; their nerves did not jerk and twitch at the enforced waiting; they had not been so highly fed with excitement as the New York boys; they did not miss the rush and hurry

Leaving the Water.

of Broadway. Their desires were curiously in character. One of them "wanted to see a stone fence once more before he was shot," and another "wanted to drink water from a well again out of a bucket." He shut his eyes and sucked in his lips at the recollection. The others all nodded gravely; they all knew they had drunk out of wooden buckets. The New York men knew nothing of stone walls. They made jokes of their discomforts, and added others from Weber & Fields, and their similes showed that they had worked when at home in the law courts, the city hospitals, and in the department stores. "The food was not exactly Shanley's," they said, and the distance across the lake was about that of the home-stretch at Morris Park. They were more restless, nervous, and argumentative than the New England men, and they, at that distance, held the Spaniard in fine contempt. They "wouldn't do a thing to him," they said. And later they certainly kept their word. The Massachusetts men were more modest. I told them that the New York men were getting up athletic sports, and running races between the athletes of the different companies.

"Oh, well," said one of the New England men, "when they find out who is their fastest runner, I'll challenge him to run away from the first Spaniard we see. I'll bet I beat him by a mile." It is a good sign when a regiment makes jokes at the expense of its courage. It is likely to be most unpleasant when the fighting begins.

It seemed a fact almost too good to be true, that the great complaint of the New York men

Second Infantry Drill at Tampa. The regiment entrenching itself (time, seven minutes).

was the superabundance of beans served out to them, and that the first complaint of the sons of Massachusetts was that they had not received beans enough. " Beans for breakfast, beans for lunch, beans for dinner—what t'ell ! " growled the New Yorkers.

" And as for beans," shrieked a Massachusetts warrior, " they don't give you enough to fill a tablespoon."

While the Second Massachusetts was in camp there was a military funeral under the pines of Lakeland when the body of Weslie S. Brass, of Company I, who died of pneumonia, was sent North. His company was detailed to escort the body to the train, but every other company in the regiment volunteered to march behind it also, and all the citizens of Lakeland lined the sandy streets and stood with heads uncovered as it passed. Before many weeks had passed men of higher rank than that of private were killed in battle, but had this boy been a major-general, or had he been killed leading a forlorn hope, no greater honor could have been shown him nor more tenderness and consideration.

The State of Florida is not very far from the Commonwealth of Massachusetts when a boy is dying under a tent, and a woman stood outside the little chapel crying because the officers had not allowed her to take the sick soldier to her own house. She was only one of many women, each of whom came to the camp to ask if she could not nurse the soldier, or bring him home with her so that she might feel that she was doing something for the cause, so that his mother up in Massachusetts might feel that some other mother had been with him at the last. Colonel Clarke knew the boy was far better off in the camp hospital than he could be in the hands of untrained nurses. So the women of Lakeland had to content themselves with robbing their own gardens and the fields of flowers for his coffin, and in joining in the procession to his funeral.

The chaplain held the service just at sunset, in a little Episcopal church set in a grove of pines at the edge of the lake. Beside the coffin a guard of honor had stood all day in white gloves and brightened brass and dustless blue, objects of cleanliness and smartness, the like of which no one had seen near Tampa for many weeks. But their presence alone was not honor enough for a Volunteer, so the Colonel came with his staff, and the regimental band followed up the hill, the drums rolling heavily and the bugles breathing a dirge, and following after them marched com-

THE ROCKING-CHAIR PERIOD

pany after company, winding out from under the trees and up the dusty road in an endless column of blue, hundreds of young soldiers, erect and clear-eyed, with clean-cut New England faces, the sons of farmers, mill-hands, lawyers, the individuality of each heightened by the uniform he wore. There was not standing-room enough in the chapel for more than a third of them, so the other companies surrounded it in long, motionless lines, while the voices of two officers and two privates, singing together, sounded through the open windows in the hush of the twilight.

> The day is spent and I am far from home,
> Lead Thou me on,

they sang, and a stillness came over the little village and upon the townspeople lining the sidewalks and leaning on the garden gates, upon the lake and the hundreds of white tents among the moss-bearing pines.

"I am the resurrection and the life," the chaplain read, and a thousand young men in blue uniform bent their heads.

It was a good sight for the people of Florida to see. It showed them all that not even one of 80,000 Volunteers can fall from the ranks either by illness or by a hostile bullet without receiving honor and attaining his reward. Weslie S. Brass was honored with a funeral that a marshal of France might have deserved and one which taught a fine lesson. It woke deep, serious thoughts in the hearts of many young men. It helped draw two little towns in far distant States close together. It showed that the man who is in uniform is the man his countrymen honor above all other men, even if he is only a private of one regiment among many. If a college professor, no matter how distinguished, had died in Lakeland, it is doubtful whether a thousand men would have asked to be allowed to march behind his body, or whether the people would have lined the streets to see it pass, or whether every mother would have wept as though for her own son. It was what Weslie Brass had volunteered to do for the Union that gained him a tribute from his countrymen in a far-away State. It was the offer of his services, and, if need be, of his life, that won him a public funeral. That he died before he saw the enemy did not count for much with his colonel, nor with his fellow-countrymen. He had started for the front, and that was enough in Westfield, Massachusetts, and in Lakeland, Florida.

The Regular soldier was professionally indif-

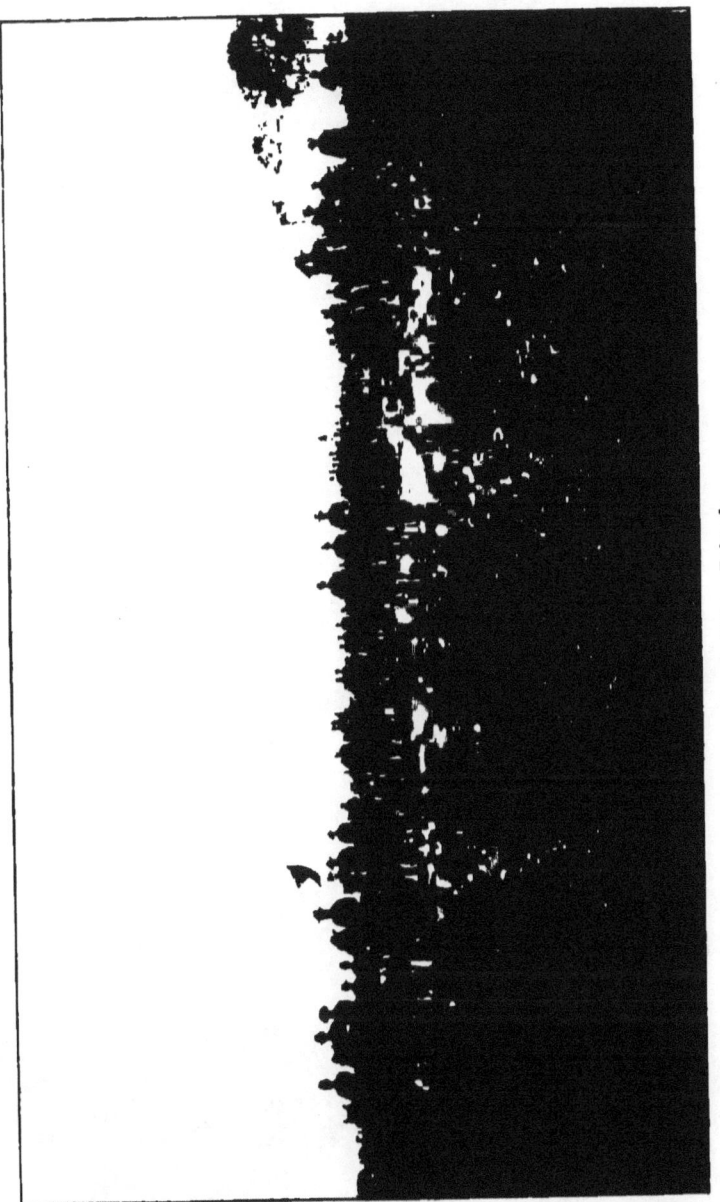

An Artillery Brigade.

ferent. He was used to camp-life, and regarded soldiering as a business. Indeed, some of them regarded it so entirely as a business, and as nothing more, that those whose time had expired in camp did not re-enlist for the war, but went off into private life in the face of it. That is where they differed from the Volunteer, who left private life the moment war came. But a great many of these time-expired Regulars did not re-enlist, because they preferred to join the Volunteers, where advancement is more rapid, and where their superior experience would soon obtain for them the rank of sergeant, or possibly a commission.

Those who did remain were as fine a looking body of soldiers as can be seen in any of the Continental regiments. Indeed, there are so few of them that the recruiting officer has only himself to blame if he fails to pick out the best, and the result of his selection is that the men of our Regular army correspond to the *corps d'élite* of European armies. Whether it was General Randolph's artillerymen firing imaginary shrapnel at imaginary foes, or the dough-boys in skirmish-line among the roots of the palmettoes, or at guard-mounting, or the cavalrymen swimming their horses, with both horse and man entirely stripped for action, the discipline was so good that it obtruded itself; and the manner in which each man handled his horse or musket, and especially himself, made you proud that they were American soldiers, and desperately sorry that there were so few of them.

An American citizen thinks the American soldier is the best, for the easy reason that he is an American; but there were three Englishmen whose profession had qualified them to know soldiers of every land, and who were quite as enthusiastic over the cavalry as any American could be. For one thing, all of our men are physically as large as Life Guardsmen, and what they lose in contrast by lack of gold and pipeclay, and through the inferiority of their equipment and uniform, is made up to them in the way they ride a horse. A German or English trooper sits his horse like a clothes-pin stuck on a line—the line may rise or sag, or swing in the wind, but the clothes-pin maintains its equilibrium at any cost, and is straight, unbending, and a thing to itself. The American trooper, with his deep saddle and long stirrup, swings with the horse, as a ship rides at anchor on the waves; he makes a line of grace and strength and suppleness from the rake of his sombrero to the toe of

Third Cavalry at Drill.

his hooded stirrup. When his horse walks, he sits it erect and motionless; when it trots, he rises with it, but never leaves the saddle; and when it gallops, he swings in unison with it like a cowboy, or a cockswain in a racing-shell.

It was a wonderful sight to see two thousand of these men advancing through the palmettoes, the red and white guidons fluttering at the fore, and the horses sweeping onward in a succession of waves, as though they were being driven forward by the wind. It will always puzzle me to know what the American people found to occupy them that was of such importance as to keep them from coming to see their own army, no matter how small it was, while it was rehearsing and drilling among the pines and palms of Florida. There will be few such chances again to see a brigade of cavalry advancing through a forest of palms in a line two miles long, and breaking up into skirmishes and Cossack outposts, with one troop at a trot and another at a walk, and others tearing, cheering through the undergrowth, their steel swords flashing over their heads and the steel horse-shoes flashing underfoot. It was a fine spectacle, and it was due to such occasional spectacles in and around the camps that the rocking-chair life was rendered bearable.

THE CUBAN AND PORTO RICAN CAMPAIGNS

But at last it came to an end, for the Commander-in-Chief finally arrived, and with him his staff in the new uniform, looking very smart and very soldierly; and all the other officers who had been suffering at Tampa, in heavy blue tunics without pockets, gazed but once upon the staff, and with envy, and then telegraphed frantically for the khaki outfit that would not come. We

"Who said oats?"

were all desperately hurried then; we had no idea where we were going, nor for how long. No secret, be it said to the credit of the censor and the staff officers, was ever better kept; but we knew, at last, that we were going, and that was joy, and the tears and rage of those who were to be left behind was a fine thing to see.

One hour we thought Santiago was the place, and the next Porto Rico, and the next we swung back to Santiago. We thought this because A, of such a staff, had told B, of another staff, who had told C, that we should take only ten days' rations. On the other hand, the Japanese military *attaché* had been told to take his tent with him; so that must mean a landing at Mariel. Still, the censor had objected to the word "spurs," so it must be Matanzas. It was all quite as absurd as that, and, as a matter of fact, no one knew up to the hour when we were ordered on board.

CHAPTER IV

THE VOYAGE OF THE TRANSPORTS

THE departure of the transports from Tampa Bay, when it came after many weary postponements and delays, was neither picturesque nor moving. The band did not play "The Girl I Left Behind Me," nor did crowds of weeping women cling to the bulkheads and wave their damp handkerchiefs; the men who were going to die for their country did not swarm in the rigging and cheer the last sight of land. They had done that on the morning of June 8th, and had been ingloriously towed back to the dock; they had done it again on the morning of June 10th, and had immediately dropped anchor a few hundred yards off shore. So they were suspicious and wary, and when the head-quarters ship, the *Segurança,* left the dock three colored women and a pathetic group of perspiring stevedores and three soldiers represented the popular interest in her departure. The largest number of United States troops that ever went down to the sea in

Port Tampa on Day of Sailing of Transports.

ships to invade a foreign country were those that formed the Fifth Army Corps when it sailed for Santiago. The thought of twelve thousand men on thirty-two troop ships and their escort of fourteen war-ships suggests the Spanish Armada.

It brings up a picture of a great flotilla, grim, sinister, and menacing, fighting its way through the waves on its errand of vengeance and conquest. But as a matter of fact the expedition bore a most distinct air of the commonplace. It moved through a succession of sparkling, sunlit days, over a sea as smooth as a lake, undisturbed by Spanish cruisers or by shells from Spanish forts. As far as the eye could see it had the ocean entirely to itself.

Scattered over a distance of seven miles the black passenger steamers and the mouse-colored war-ships steamed in three uneven columns and suggested a cluster of excursion steamers, and yachts and tugs as one sees them coming back from Sandy Hook after an international yacht-race.

The troop-ships were fitted up with pine cots and a small proportion of stalls for the horses; the first-class cabins were turned over to the officers. On some of them the men swarmed over every part of the ship, on others the officers held only the bridge to themselves.

Probably half of the men forming the expedition had never been to sea before. They probably will desire never to go again, but will say from the depth of their one experience that the dangers of the deep are vastly exaggerated. They will not wish to go again, because their first experience was more full of discomfort than any other trip they are likely to take could possibly be; on the other hand, they may sail the seas many times before they find it as smooth, or the rain as infrequent, the sun as beautiful, or the heavens as magnificent.

We travelled at the rate of seven miles an hour, with long pauses for thought and consultation. Sometimes we moved at the rate of four miles an hour, and frequently we did not move at all. Our delays were chiefly due to the fact that two of the steamers were each towing a great scow or lighter, on which the troops were to be conveyed to shore, and because another one was towing a schooner filled with water. The speed of the squadron was, of course, the speed of the slowest ship in it, so the water-boat set the pace.

The war-ships treated us with the most punctilious courtesy and concealed contempt. And we certainly deserved it. We could not keep in line and we lost ourselves and each other, and the gun-boats and torpedo-boats were kept busy rounding us up, and giving us sharp, precise orders in passing, through a megaphone, to which either

Generals Miles and Shafter on Deck of the Transport *Segurança* at Port Tampa.

nobody on board made any reply, or everyone did. The gun-boats were like swift, keen-eyed, intelligent collies rounding up a herd of bungling sheep. They looked so workmanlike and clean, and the men were so smart in their white duck, that the soldiers cheered them all along the line, as they dashed up and down it, waving their wig-wags frantically.

The life on board the head-quarters ship was uneventful for those who were not in command. For these their tables and desks were spread in the "social hall," and all day long they worked busily and mysteriously on maps and lists and orders, and six typewriters banged on their machines until late at night. The ship was greatly overcrowded; it held all of General Shafter's staff, all of General Breckinridge's staff, the Cuban generals, the officers and five hundred men of the First Regiment, all the foreign *attachés*, and an army of stenographers, secretaries, clerks, servants, couriers, valets, and colored waiters.

All of these were jumbled together. There were three cane chairs with seats and two cane chairs without seats. If you were so unlucky as not to capture one of these, you clung sidewise to the bench around the ship's rail or sat on the deck. At no one moment were you alone. Your most intimate conversation was overheard by everyone, whether he wished to do so or not; the *attachés* could not compare notes on our deficiencies without being betrayed, nor could the staff

THE VOYAGE OF THE TRANSPORTS

Artillery for Cuba.

discuss its plan of campaign without giving it to the whole ship. Seven different languages were in course of constant circulation, and the grievances of the servants and the badinage of the colored cooks mingled with the latest remarks on the war. At night you picked your way over prostrate forms of soldiers and of overworked stewards, who toiled eighteen hours a day in a temperature of 102 degrees.

The water on board the ship was so bad that it could not be used for purposes of shaving. It smelled like a frog-pond or a stable-yard, and it tasted as it smelt. Before we started from Tampa Bay the first time it was examined by the doctors, who declared that in spite of the bad smell and taste it was not unhealthy, but Colonel J. J. Astor offered to pay for fresh water, for which Plant charged two cents a gallon, if they would empty all of the bad-smelling water overboard. General Shafter said it was good enough for him, and Colonel Astor's very considerate offer was not accepted. So we all drank apollinaris water or tea. The soldiers, however, had to drink the water furnished them, except those who were able to pay five cents a glass to the ship's porter, who had a private supply of good water which he made into lemonade. The ship's crew and engineers used this water.

Before handing the ship over to the Government, the company removed all of her wine stock and table-linen, took out two of her dining-tables and generally stripped her, and then sent her South undermanned. Her steward hired and borrowed and bought linen and servants and table-waiters at Tampa, but there was so little linen

Waiting for the Expedition to Move.

that it was seldom changed, and had it not been that the servants of the officers were willing to help wait at table, there would have been four stewards to look after the wants of fifty or sixty passengers. The food supplied by the line to which the ship belonged was villanous; the enlisted men forward were much better served by the Government with good beans, corned beef, and coffee. Apparently, no contract or agreement as to quantity or quality of food for the officers had been made by the Government with the owners.

The squadron at night, with the lights showing from every part of the horizon, made one think he was entering a harbor, or leaving one. But by day we seemed adrift on a sea as untravelled as it was when Columbus first crossed it. On the third day out we saw Romano Key. It was the first sight of land, and after that from time to time we made out a line of blue mountains on the starboard side. The squadron, though, had apparently been sighted from the shore, for the light-houses along the coast were dark at night, which would seem to show that the lesson of the Armada has not been lost on the Spaniard.

Someone has said that "God takes care of drunken men, sailors, and the United States." This expedition apparently relied on the probability that that axiom would prove true. "The luck of the British Army," of which Mr. Kipling boasts, is the luck of Job in comparison to the good fortune that pursued that expedition. There was really nothing to prevent a Spanish torpedo-boat from running out and sinking four or five ships while they were drifting along, spread out over the sea at such distance that the vessels in the rear were lost to sight for fourteen hours at a

General Miles on the Day of Sailing of Transports.

time, and no one knew whether they had sunk or had been blown up, or had grown disgusted and gone back home. As one of the generals on board said, "This is God Almighty's war, and we are only His agents."

The foreign *attachés* regarded the fair weather that accompanied us, the brutal good health of the men, the small loss of horses and mules, and the entire freedom from interference on the part of the enemy with the same grudging envy that one watches a successful novice winning continuously at roulette. At night the fleet was as conspicuous as Brooklyn or New York, with the lights of the Bridge included, but the Spanish took no advantage of that fact; no torpedo-destroyers slipped out from Cardenas or Nuevitas, or waited for us in the old Bahama Channel, where for twelve miles the ships were crowded into a channel only seven miles across. Of course, our own escort would have finished them if they had, but not before they could have thrown torpedoes right and left into the helpless hulks of the transports, and given us a loss to remember even greater than that of the *Maine*.

But as it was, nothing happened. We rolled along at our own pace, with the lights the navy had told us to extinguish blazing defiantly to the stars, with bands banging out rag-time music, and with the foremost vessels separated sometimes for half a day at a time from the laggards in the rear.

It was a most happy-go-lucky expedition, run

THE VOYAGE OF THE TRANSPORTS

Transports Off for Cuba.

with real American optimism and readiness to take big chances, and with the spirit of a people who recklessly trust that it will come out all right in the end, and that the barely possible may not happen, that the joker may not turn up to spoil the hand, who risk grade crossings and all that they imply, who race transatlantic steamers through a fog for the sake of a record, and who on this occasion certainly "enchred God's almighty storm and bluffed the eternal sea."

No one complained and no one grumbled. The soldiers turned over to sleep on the bare decks, with final injunctions not to be awakened for anything under a Spanish battle-ship, and whenever the ships drew up alongside, the men bombarded each other with jokes on the cheerful fact that they were hungry and thirsty and sore for sleep. But, for all that, our army's greatest invasion of a foreign land was completely successful, but chiefly so, one cannot help thinking, because the Lord looks after his own.

There are three places in the West Indies where Columbus is said to have first landed; one of them is at Santiago. Some hundreds of years from now there will probably be as great a dispute as to where the American troops first landed when they came to drive the Spaniard across the sea and to establish the republic of Cuba. There were two "first landings" of the army of invasion; but before it came to Cuba soldiers of the Regular Army were put ashore at Arbolitas Point, when they

THE VOYAGE OF THE TRANSPORTS

General Shafter at Port Tampa Superintending Embarkation.

acted as an escort to the *Gussie* expedition. On this occasion a Spanish lieutenant and several of his soldiers were killed, and on the American side a correspondent was shot through the arm. Still another landing was made before the Regulars came in force, this time by marines, at Guantanamo Bay; and as they established a camp there and remained on shore, the credit of first raising the American flag on Cuban soil, and of keeping it in its place, belongs to them, and through them to the navy. The first American flag raised temporarily was put up on a block-house near Cardenas by Lieutenant Willard, also of the navy.

When the army came at last, sixteen thousand strong, in thirty-one transports, and with an escort of fourteen war-ships, it made two landings: a preliminary one on June 20th, when only twenty people went ashore at Aserraderos, and on June 22d at Baiquiri, when all through the day there was a continuous going and coming of shore-boats from the transports, each carrying from twenty to thirty men, and following after each other as swiftly as cable-cars on Broadway.

The preliminary landing was made by General Shafter and Admiral Sampson without any escort or protection from United States troops.

The *Segurança* ran away from the rest of the troop-ships on the morning of June 20th. Captain Chadwick, Commander of the *New York*, had come over the side when we were twenty miles from Santiago, and Admiral Sampson had followed him. When the ship was within five miles of Morro Castle they conferred with General Shafter in his cabin and decided that he should go ashore at Aserraderos at once to see General Garcia and discuss the question of a landing-place for the army.

So we abandoned the transports altogether and steamed off selfishly to make the first landing of the expedition alone. It was an interesting landing in every way, and especially so as I have said, because it was made without the escort or protection of any American troops. Only four boatloads left the ship, carrying only thirty of her six hundred passengers.

Among these were Generals Shafter and Ludlow, Colonels McClernand, Astor, and Wagner, Lieutenants Miley and Noble, Captain Stewart Brice, Captain Lee, of the British Army, Captain Count von Goetzen, of the German Army, General Castillo, of the Cuban Army, and Admiral Sampson and Lieutenant Staunton, of the *New York*, and Frederic Remington, Caspar Whitney, Stephen Bonsal, and the writer.

The landing was made in a little bay overhung by a grove of cocoa-nut palms at the base of a great range of mountains eighteen miles west of Santiago. The mountains stretched back from the jungle of manigua bushes on the coast until they met the clouds. There was no sign of life or of man's habitation on any part of their great terraces except where here and there a cattle trail zigzagged up and down across the valleys.

Admiral Sampson and General Shafter Going Ashore at Aserraderos.

Drawn up under the cocoa-nut palms were a double row of Cuban officers, and as the blue-jackets drove the long-boat from the *Vixen* toward the shore, the Cubans dashed into the water up to their waists and came toward us, cheering and shouting, and the officers on horseback surrounded the boat, splashing and churning up the water, and saluting the two men whose coming meant for them the freedom and independence of their island.

It was a remarkable and most dramatic picture. In the background were the towering, grim green mountains, with their tops lost in the clouds, the motionless palms and the ragged, half-naked foot-soldiers crowding far into the water, and in the foreground the white long-boat, with her crew of blue-jackets and with the American flag fluttering at the stern.

There were mules and ponies waiting for the commanding officers, and, as the shore-boats from the *Segurança* were rowed after them into the cove, they disappeared up the trail, surrounded by the mounted escorts. There was no cavalry escort to guide us, so our boats promptly ran aground on a shoal, and the Cuban patriots dashed into the water up to their waists and carried us ashore on their shoulders.

The picture presented by Captain Stewart Brice, late city Councilman of Greater New York and now of the Volunteer Army, clasping a naked negro around the neck and digging him in the stomach with his spurs, was one that would have made his fellow-members of Tammany Hall proud.

The trail up the mountain to Garcia's camp was steep and rough, but the fresh, pungent odor of earth and grass and trees, after the stuffy,

Captain Stewart Brice Being Carried Ashore at Aserraderos.

sweating decks of the overcrowded troop-ship, made the climbing easy.

It was pathetic and beautiful to see with what eagerness and tender anxiety the Cubans and negroes combined to welcome the American officers and to cater to their entertainment out of their own absolute want and poverty. It was not enough that they stood in salute to the General in two long lines from the place of his arrival until he had reached their camp, but they brought us the milk of cocoa-nut and limes, and mangoes and pineapples, and made coffee and offered us water, and forced us to mount on their half-starved horses, while they walked.

The conference of the powers was held under a thatched roof of palm-leaves that drooped over the sides, making four hanging walls. Under this sat General Shafter, in his blue blouse, with its double rows of buttons that mark the major-general; Admiral Sampson, in fresh white duck, and General Garcia, in a slouch hat and linen uniform, with high military boots.

Garcia is a handsome man, with a white mustache and goatee, and looks like Caprivi, the German Chancellor. In his forehead, between the snow-white eyebrows, is a deep bullet wound, which shows where he tried to kill himself when, ten years ago, he was a prisoner in the hands of the Spaniards.

It had been a long, hard, and desperate struggle for the white-haired old soldier, and as he sat at last in his own camp, with the Admiral of the

Atlantic Squadron on his right and the American General on his left, he must have thought that at last his reward had come.

Apart from its political value, the scene was one of wonderful tropical beauty. It was worthy of a meeting of such importance in the history of the Republic of Cuba and to the great Republic across the Florida Straits.

Beneath the camp the sea stretched in a motionless plain of dark blue, lying pulseless in the heat; overhead the mountains rose through a misty haze of heat to meet clouds of a glaring, blinding white. Every feature of the landscape was painted in high lights; there was no shading, it was all brilliant, gorgeous, and glaring.

The sea was an indigo blue, like the blue in a washtub; the green of the mountains was the green of corroded copper; the scarlet trees were the red of a Tommy's jacket, and the sun was like a lime-light in its fierceness.

While the great men talked under the palm-trees, the Americans and the Cubans made each other's acquaintance, and the blue-jackets mixed with the barefooted soldiers, and the two *attachés* made snap-shot photographs for the education of the British and German armies. Their presence with the invading army filled the officers of the

Generals Shafter and Garcia with Cuban Volunteers.

Cuban Army with an idea that their struggle for liberty was stirring the nations of the world.

When they heard that on the *Segurança* were also military *attachés* from as far afield as Japan, they could not express their surprise, and when they learned that there was one from Austria as well, they could not understand it at all. Austria, they argued, was helping Spain, so they could not comprehend why one of that nation was allowed with the American Army, but they satisfied themselves at last by arguing that Captain Lee, the British *attaché*, was there to look after the Cuban interests, and in case Austria interfered, to order out the British Army.

It was the first time we had seen the Cuban revolutionists in the field, and what impressed us most favorably was the appearance of the officers. They were fine-looking, young gentlemen, well, and even smartly, uniformed, and with the bearing and assurance of officers and of men accustomed to command. Their soldiers were ragged and half-starved, and inadequately armed, but they obeyed the few commands we heard given them correctly, and showed a rudimentary grasp of company drill and discipline. They spent the time given to the conference in studying the new-comers with cheerful curiosity, but their officers went on about their duties without wasting time on men who did not for the moment concern them.

When the conference was ended a line of Cuban soldiers again lined the trail for General Shafter's return, and to the sound of calls on the trumpets, and to presented arms, he rode back to his boat, and the first landing of the first detachment of the American army of invasion had been successfully accomplished.

The landing in force took place the second day after this at nine o'clock in the morning. All we had been told was that the landing would take place at daybreak, and at that hour we woke to find the transports drawn up in their usual disorder opposite the town of Nueva Salamanca, which lies eighteen miles east of Santiago. Just above this village is the river Baiquiri, and it was this river and not the town that gave its name to the landing-place. We watched the landing from the decks of the *Segurança*, which in order that General Shafter might the better direct the landing, was the ship that ran in closest to the shore. To better understand what followed, the reader might know what we did not know—the plan of operations as it was prepared beforehand. The full plot is given in the bulletin from the

THE VOYAGE OF THE TRANSPORTS

flag-ship *New York*, issued on the day before the landing, which the newspapers have already frequently printed. Some of its most important orders were as follows :

NORTH ATLANTIC STATION, U. S. FLAG-SHIP NEW YORK (1st Rate),

Off Santiago de Cuba, June 21, 1898.

ORDER OF BATTLE.

1.—The Army Corps will land to-morrow morning, the entire force landing at Baiquiri. The landing will begin at daylight, or as soon thereafter as practicable. General Castillo, with a thousand men coming from the eastward of Baiquiri, will assist in clearing the way for an unopposed landing, by flanking out the Spanish forces at that point.

2.—Simultaneously with the shelling of the beach and block-houses at Baiquiri, the Ensenada de los Altares, and Aguadores, both to the eastward of Santiago, and the small Bay of Cabáñas, about two and one-half miles to the westward of Santiago, will be shelled by the ships stationed there for that purpose.

3.—A feint in force of landing at Cabáñas will be made, about ten of the transports, the last to disembark their forces at Baiquiri, remaining during the day, or greater part of the day, about two miles to the southward of Cabáñas, lowering boats and making apparent preparations for disembarking a large body of troops ; at the same time General Rabi with five hundred Cuban troops will make a demonstration on the west side of Cabáñas.

4.—The following vessels are assigned to bombard the four points mentioned above :

At Cabáñas, the *Scorpion*, *Vixen*, and *Texas*.

At Aguadores, the *Eagle* and *Gloucester*.

At Ensenada de los Altares, the *Hornet*, *Helena*, and *Bancroft*.

THE CUBAN AND PORTO RICAN CAMPAIGNS

At Baiquiri, the *Detroit, Castine, Wasp,* and *New Orleans,* the *Detroit* and *Castine* on the westward flank, the *Wasp* and *New Orleans* on the eastern flank. All the vessels named will be in their position at daylight.

. . . .

6.—The *Texas* and *Brooklyn* will exchange blockading stations, the *Texas* going inside to be near Cabáñas. The *Brooklyn, Massachusetts, Iowa,* and *Oregon* will retain their blockading positions, and will keep a vigilant watch on the harbor mouth. The *Indiana* will take the *New Orleans's* position in the blockading line east of Santiago, and between the flagship *New York* and the shore. This is only a temporary assignment for the *Indiana,* to strengthen the blockading line during the landing, and avoid any possibility of the enemy's breaking through should he attempt to get out of the port.

7.—The *Suwanee, Osceola,* and *Wompatuck* will be prepared to tow boats. Each will be provided with two five or six-inch lines, one on each quarter; each long enough to take in tow a dozen or more boats.

8.—These vessels will report at the *New York* at 3.30 A.M. on June 22d, prepared to take in tow the ships' boats which are to assist in the landing of troops and convey them to Baiquiri.

9.—The *Texas, Brooklyn, Massachusetts, Iowa, Oregon, New York,* and *Indiana* will send all their steam-cutters and all their pulling boats, with the exception of one retained on board each ship, to assist in the landing. These boats will report at the *New York* at 3 A.M.

10.—Each boat, whaleboat, and cutter will have three men; each launch five men, and each steam-cutter its full crew and an officer for their own management. In addition to these men, each boat will carry five men, including one capable of acting as coxswain to manage and direct the transports' boats. Each steam-launch will be in charge of an officer, who will report to Captain Goodrich. Care will be taken in the selection of boat-keepers and coxswains, to take no men who are gun-pointers or who occupy positions of special importance at the battery.

. . . .

14.—The attention of Commanding Officers of all vessels engaged in blockading Santiago de Cuba is earnestly called to the necessity of the utmost vigilance from this time forward—both as to maintaining stations and readiness for action, and as to keeping a close watch upon the harbor-mouth. If the Spanish Admiral ever intends to attempt to escape, that attempt will be made soon.

WILLIAM T. SAMPSON,
Rear Admiral, Commander-in-Chief, U. S. Naval Force, North Atlantic Station.

At Baiquiri are the machine-shops and ore-dock of the Spanish-American Iron Company. The ore-dock runs parallel with the coast-line, and back of it are the machine-shop and the company's corrugated zinc-shacks and rows of native huts thatched with palm-leaves. Behind these rise the mountains, and on a steep and lofty spur is a little Spanish block-house with a flag-pole at its side. As the sun rose and showed this to the waiting fleet it is probable that every one of the thousands of impatient soldiers had the same thought, that the American flag must wave over the blockhouse before the sun sank again.

The morning broke cool and clear. There was no sign of life in the village, and, except that the machine-shop and one of a long row of ore-cars on the ore-pier were on fire and blazing briskly, we should have thought that the place was deserted. Until nine o'clock nothing happened, and then from Siboney came the first sounds of bombardment. It is probable that to ninety per cent. of the soldiers it was the first shot they had ever heard fired in anger. There was another long wait while the launches sped from ship to ship with shore-boats rocking in tow on cables behind them, and in time they were filled, but not without much mirth and a few accidents.

It was delightful to see the fine scorn of the coxswains as the "dough-boys" fell and jumped and tumbled from the gangway ladder into the heaving boats, that dropped from beneath them like a descending elevator or rose suddenly and threw them on their knees. It was much more dangerous than anyone imagined, for later in the day when two men of the Twenty-fifth Regiment were upset at the pier, the weight of the heavy cartridge-belt and haversack and blanket-roll carried them to the bottom. Soon the sea was dotted with rows of white boats filled with men bound about with white blanket-rolls and with muskets at all angles, and as they rose and fell on the water and the newspaper yachts and transports crept in closer and closer, the scene was strangely suggestive of a boat-race, and one almost waited for the starting gun.

It came at last, though in a different spirit, from the *New Orleans*, and in an instant the *Detroit*, the *Castine*, and the little *Wasp* were enveloped in smoke. The valleys sent back the reports of the guns in long, thundering echoes that reverberated again and again, and the mountain-side began at once to spurt up geysers of earth and branches of broken bushes, as though someone had stabbed it with a knife and the blood had spurted from the wound. But there were no answering shots, and under the cover of the smoke the long-boats and launches began to scurry toward the shore. Meanwhile, the warships kept up their fierce search for hidden batteries, tearing off the tin roofs of the huts, dismantling the block-houses, and sending the thatched shacks into bonfires of flame. The men in the boats pulled harder at the oars, the steam-launches rolled and pitched, tugging at the weight behind them, and the first convoy of five hundred men were soon bunched together, racing bow by bow for the shore. A launch turned suddenly and steered for a long pier under the ore-docks, the waves lifted it to the level of the pier, and a half-dozen men leaped through the air and landed on the pier-head, waving their muskets above them. At the same moment two of the other boats were driven through the surf to the beach itself, and the men tumbled out and scrambled to their feet upon the shore of Cuba. In an instant a cheer rose faintly from the shore, and more loudly from the

A Cheer by the Rough Riders.

war-ships. It was caught up by every ship in the transport fleet, and was carried for miles over the ocean. Men waved their hats, and jumped up and down, and shrieked as though they themselves had been the first to land, and the com-

THE VOYAGE OF THE TRANSPORTS

bined cheering seemed as though it must surely reach to the walls of Santiago and tell the enemy that the end was near. But the cheers were whispers to what came later, when, outlined against the sky, we saw four tiny figures scaling the sheer face of the mountain up the narrow trail to the highest block-house. For a moment they were grouped together there at the side of the Spanish fort, and then thousands of feet above the shore the American flag was thrown out against the sky, and the sailors on the men-of-war, the Cubans, and our own soldiers in the village, the soldiers in the long-boats, and those still hanging to the sides and ratlines of the troop-ships, shouted and cheered again, and every steam-whistle on the ocean for miles about shrieked and tooted and roared in a pandemonium of delight and pride and triumph.

CHAPTER V

THE GUASIMAS FIGHT

THE problems which presented themselves to the commanding general of the Santiago expedition might be placed in a list, as follows:

1. To disembark 12,000 men, artillery, and supplies from thirty-two transports.

2. To move the men, rations, ammunition, and artillery toward Santiago, up a steep and narrow trail through a wooded country.

3. To reconnoitre the approach to Santiago, to clear away any forces which might retard the advance of the army upon it, and, finally, to take Santiago by assault, or by siege.

The selection of a landing-place for the army was one much discussed, and, possibly, Siboney and Baiquiri were as suitable for the purpose as any of the others might have been, but when we recollect the original purpose of the expedition they seem unnecessarily distant from the seat of the proposed operations. The original reason for sending an army to Santiago was a somewhat pe-

THE GUASIMAS FIGHT

culiar one. It was because our war-ships could not reach the war-ships of the enemy. It has often happened that an army has asked the navy to assist it in an assault upon a fortified port. But

Colonel Roosevelt.

this is probably the only instance when a fleet has called upon an army to capture another fleet. Cervera and his ships of war lay bottled up in Santiago harbor, and on account of the forts and mines which guarded the approach to the inner harbor, our vessels could not reach him. Accordingly, the army was asked to attack these forts in the rear, to capture them, to cut the wires con-

Colonel Roosevelt and Richard Harding Davis.

necting them with the mines in the harbor, and so clear the way for our fleet to enter and do battle with the enemy.

To carry out this programme, the army might have landed at Aguadores, on the east of the

THE GUASIMAS FIGHT

mouth of the harbor of Santiago, and at Cabáñas, on the west. Each of these ports is but three miles in the rear of the batteries which guard the entrance to the harbor. To convey troops, and artillery, and rations three miles would not have been a difficult problem. Or, had the navy decided against Aguadores as a suitable landing-place, it would still have been possible to have made the landing at Siboney, and then marched the troops along the railroad which clings to the coast from Siboney to Aguadores, under the shelter of a steep range of cliffs. This advance could have been made safely under the cover of the guns of the fleet. No Spanish force could have lived on the railroad, or on the cliffs above it, under such a fire. It has been argued that had the army approached Santiago from Aguadores, a road of retreat for the Spanish garrison would have been left uncovered. This was equally true of the place selected for the actual attack, which left the road of retreat to Holguin open until July 8th. For other reasons, however, the landing was made at Baiquiri, eighteen miles away from the harbor, and the point of attack was not the forts, but the city itself. Further, the attack was made at a time when the city was protected by Cervera's guns, and in the face of the fact that he had declared if the Americans succeeded in entering the city, he would instantly bombard it, and so render it untenable, which he could very easily have done. When General Nelson A. Miles arrived he decided that the attack on the forts was even then the proper method to

Landing of American Forces at Siboney.

pursue in order to capture the city, and he ordered General Guy Henry to reconnoitre Cabáñas, and prepare to land artillery. General Henry made the reconnoissance, but before further movement was ordered, the surrender of Santiago, which had been made necessary by the departure of Cervera from the harbor, and by the capture of the hills overlooking the city by our army, was an accomplished fact.

The disembarkment at Baiquiri was a marvellous and wonderful thing. Only two men were drowned. What makes this so remarkable is the fact that the boats carrying the men were run up through the surf, and either beached, or brought to a pier so high that to reach it the men had to jump from the boat at the exact moment it rose on the wave. Seven thousand men were put ashore in this way. The greater part of the pier was covered with loose boards, and the men walked on these or stepped across open girders, two feet apart. While doing this, they carried their packs, arms, and ammunition. Three weeks later, when I returned to this pier with General Miles, then on his way to Porto Rico, the loose boards were still loose, and he landed in the same way, by scrambling up the pier as the boat rose, and picked his way over the same open girders. During those three weeks thousands of men, thousands of tons of supplies, and thousands of boxes of ammunition had been piled up high upon this pier, and carried away from it, and yet, apparently, no attempt had been made to render it safe, either for the arms or for the men. It was still impossible to cross it without running the risk of stepping into space, or of treading on the end of a loose board and falling between the girders. It was obviously the work of the engineers to improve this wharf, or build a better one. But the engineers happened to be on board the transport *Alamo*, and on the day of landing General Shaf-

Another View of the Landing.

ter sent the *Alamo* to Aserraderos for three days to build pontoon bridges for the Cubans. In consequence, the men whose services at that time were most greatly needed, were thirty-six miles up the coast, employed as ferrymen for our Cuban allies.

At Siboney matters were rather worse, as there

THE GUASIMAS FIGHT

was not even a pier as inadequate as that at Baiquiri. There the men were dumped out into the surf and waded for the shore. After several days a pier was begun, but it also was washed by the waves, and only lighters and tugs could approach it. This made it necessary to handle the supplies four or five times, instead of landing them directly from the transports on a pier big enough, and in water deep enough, to allow the transports to draw up alongside.

To add to the confusion which retarded the landing of supplies, the transport captains acted with an independence and in disregard of what was required of them, that should, early in the day, have led to their being placed in irons. The misconduct of the transport captains was so important a matter that much more space must be devoted to it than can be allowed here. In a word, they acted entirely in what they believed to be the interests of the "Owners," meaning, not the Government, which was paying them enormous rents per day, but the men who employed them in time of peace. For the greater part of each day these men kept from three to twenty miles out at sea, where it was impossible to communicate with them, and where they burned coal at the expense of the Government. Had they been given stations and ordered to anchor over them, they could have been found when the supplies they carried were wanted, and the cost of coal saved. I was on six different transports, and on none of them did I find a captain who was, in his attitude toward the Government, anything but insolent, un-American, and mutinous, and when there was any firing of any sort on shore they showed themselves to be the most abject cowards and put to the open sea, carrying the much-needed supplies with them.

When our war-ships had destroyed the *Maria Teresa*, and four hundred of her Spanish crew were clinging to the wreck, the captain of one of the transports refused to lower his boats and go to their aid. This was after the firing had entirely ceased, and there was no danger. Had it not been for the *Gloucester*, which had just been engaged with the enemy, and her two small shore-boats, the entire four hundred prisoners would have been washed into the sea, and drowned. The English Government pays the merchant vessels it uses for transports ten per cent. over their usual freight rates; our Government paid these transports two hundred to three hundred per cent. over freight rates, possibly because our Government, like nature, is not economical, and for

Major Major Major-Gen. Chaplain Colonel Lieut.-Colonel
Dunn. Brodie. Jos. Wheeler. H. A. Brown. Leonard Wood. Theodore Roosevelt.

the reason that many of the vessels were passenger-carriers, as well as freighters. But the greater number of the owners, before sending their vessels south, stripped them of everything needed on a passenger-ship, even of bed-linen and towels, and sent them to sea undermanned, so they were virtually nothing but freight-carriers and ocean tramps. The fact that this floating collection of stores was in shore one day, and out of sight twenty miles at sea the next, was one of the causes of the failure to supply the troops with rations. These captains knew that the soldiers at the front needed food, and that the food needed was in the hulls of the ships they commanded, but in order to save the owners a smashed davit, or a scratched hull, or for no other reason than their own will, they allowed the men at the front to starve while they beat up and down as they pleased.

Had there been a strong man in command of the expedition, he would have ordered them into place, stern and bow anchors would have kept them there, and a signal officer on shore could have communicated with them at their different stations in the harbor. But there was no Captain of the Port appointed, and instead of a Signal Officer to wig-wag to them, the transports were chased over many miles of sea in small row-boats. The transport captains were civilians for the time being, under the direction of the Government, and were amenable to military laws. When the stevedores mutinied at Guanica, and at the Port of Ponce, under General Miles, they were given three minutes to resume work, with the choice of being put in irons if they did not, and were informed if they jumped overboard and tried to escape, they would be shot in the water as deserters.

This inability to keep the transports near the shore, and the inexcusable failure to build a wharf on which to land supplies, explains why the rations came so slowly to the front. To get them there was the first problem of the Commanding General, and each succeeding day, as the tide rose higher, and the surf became more dangerous, it continued to confront him with graver insistence.

The first accounts of the fight of the Rough Riders at Guasimas came from correspondents three miles away at Siboney, who received their information from the wounded when they were carried to the rear, and from an officer who stampeded before the fight had fairly begun. These men declared they had been entrapped in an ambush, that Colonel Wood was dead, and that their comrades were being shot to pieces. When the newspapers reached the front, it was evident that the version these wounded men gave of the fight had been generally accepted in the States as the true account of what had occurred, and Colonel Wood and Lieutenant-Colonel Roosevelt, while praised for their courage, were condemned editorially for having advanced into the enemy's country without proper military precautions, for rushing blindly into an ambuscade, and through their "recklessness" and "foolhardiness" sacrificing the lives of their men.

Indeed, one Congressman, who from the marble rotunda of the Capitol was able to master a military problem in a Cuban swamp two thousand miles away, declared that Roosevelt ought to be court-martialled.

It is quite true that the fight was a fight against an enemy in ambush; in a country with such advantages for ambush as this, the Spaniards would be fools to fight us in any other way, but there is a vast difference between blundering into an ambuscade and setting out with a full knowledge that you will find the enemy in ambush, and finding him, there and then driving him out of his ambush and before you for a mile and a half into a full retreat. This is what Major-General Joseph Wheeler planned that General Young and Colonel Wood should do; so if the conduct of these officers was reckless, it was recklessness due to their

Captain O'Neill of the Rough Riders, also Mayor of Prescott, Ariz. Killed at San Juan.

following out the carefully prepared orders of a veteran general.

At the time of this fight General Wheeler was in command of all troops on shore, and so continued as long as General Shafter remained on board

THE GUASIMAS FIGHT

the flag-ship. What orders he gave then were in consequence final, but in starting General Young and Colonel Wood to the front when he did, he disarranged the original order in which the troops were to move forward, as it had been laid down by General Shafter before the transports arrived at Baiquiri. According to this original plan, General Lawton's division of infantry should have been in the van, and in pushing forward regiments from his own division of dismounted cavalry General Wheeler possibly exceeded his authority. That, however, is entirely a question between the two major-generals and does not concern either General Young or Colonel Wood, who merely obeyed the orders of their superior officer. The fact that the Rough Riders, in their anxiety to be well forward, had reached Siboney by making a forced march at night, does not alter the fact that their next forward movement on Guasimas was not made in a spirit of independence, but by order of the Commanding General.

On the afternoon of June 23d a Cuban officer informed General Wheeler that the enemy were intrenched at Guasimas, blocking the way to Santiago. Guasimas is not a village, nor even a collection of houses; it is the meeting-place of two trails which join at the apex of a V, three miles from the seaport town of Siboney, and continue merged in a single trail to Santiago. General Wheeler, accompanied by Cubans, reconnoitred this trail on the afternoon of the 23d, and with the position of the enemy fully explained to him, returned to Siboney and informed General Young and Colonel Wood that he would attack the place on the following morning. The plan was discussed while I was present, so I know that so far from anyone's running into an ambush unaware, every one of the officers concerned had a full knowledge of where he was to go to find the enemy, and what he was to do when he got there. No one slept that night, for until two o'clock in the morning troops were still being disembarked in the surf, and two ships of war had their search-lights turned on the landing-place, and made Siboney as light as a ball-room. Back of the search-lights was an ocean white with moonlight, and on the shore red camp-fires, at which the half-drowned troops were drying their uniforms, and the Rough Riders, who had just marched in from Baiquiri, were cooking their coffee and bacon. Below the former home of the Spanish comandante, which General Wheeler had made his head-quarters, lay the camp of the Rough Riders, and through it Cuban officers were riding their half-starved ponies, scattering the ashes of the camp-fires, and galloping over the tired bodies of the men with that courtly grace and consideration for Americans which invariably marks the Cuban gentleman. Below them was the beach and the roaring surf, in which a thousand or so naked men were assisting and impeding the progress shoreward of their comrades, in pontoons and shore-boats, which were being hurled at the beach like sleds down a water-chute.

It was one of the most weird and remarkable scenes of the war, probably of any war. An army was being landed on an enemy's coast at the dead of night, but with somewhat more of cheers and shrieks and laughter than rise from the bathers in the surf at Coney Island on a hot Sunday. It was a pandemonium of noises. The men still to be landed from the "prison hulks," as they called the transports, were singing in chorus, the men already on shore were dancing naked around the camp-fires on the beach, or shouting with delight as they plunged into the first bath that had offered in seven days, and those in the launches as they were pitched head-first at the soil of Cuba, signalized their arrival by howls of triumph. On either side rose black overhanging ridges, in the lowland between were white tents and burning fires, and from the ocean came the blazing, dazzling eyes of the search-lights shaming the quiet moonlight.

The Rough Riders left camp after three hours' troubled sleep at five in the morning. With the exception of half a dozen officers they were dis-

American Boats Landing Cubans at Siboney.

mounted, and carried their blanket-rolls, haversacks, ammunition, and carbines. General Young had already started toward Guasimas the First and Tenth dismounted Cavalry, and according to the agreement of the night before had taken the eastern trail to our right, while the Rough Riders climbed the steep ridge above Siboney and started toward the rendezvous along the trail to the west, which was on high ground and a half mile to a mile distant from the trail along which General Young was marching. There was a valley between us, and the bushes were so thick on both sides of our trail that it was not possible at any time, until we met at Guasimas, to distinguish his column.

As soon as the Rough Riders had reached the top of the ridge not twenty minutes after they had left camp, which was the first opportunity that presented itself, Colonel Wood took the precautions he was said to have neglected. He ordered Captain Capron to proceed with his troop in front of the column as an advance guard, and to choose a "point" of five men skilled as scouts and trailers. Still in advance of these he placed two Cuban scouts. The column then continued along the trail in single file. The Cubans were just at a distance of two hundred and fifty yards; the "point" of five picked men under Sergeant Byrne and duty-Sergeant Fish followed them at a distance of a hundred yards, and then came Capron's troop of sixty men strung out in single file. No flankers were placed for the reason that the dense undergrowth and the tangle of vines that stretched from the branches of the trees to the bushes below made it a physical impossibility for man or beast to move forward except along the beaten trail.

Colonel Wood rode at the head of the column, followed by two regular army officers who were members of General Wheeler's staff, a Cuban officer, and Lieutenant-Colonel Roosevelt. They rode slowly in consideration of the troopers on foot, who carried heavy burdens under a cruelly hot sun. To those who did not have to walk it was not unlike a hunting excursion in our West; the scenery was beautiful and the view down the valley one of luxuriant peace. Roosevelt had never been in the tropics and Captain McCormick and I were talking back at him over our shoulders and at each other, pointing out unfamiliar trees and birds. Roosevelt thought it looked like a good deer country, as it once was; it reminded McCormick of southern California; it looked to me like the trail across Honduras. They advanced, talking in that fashion and in high spirits, and congratulating themselves in being shut of the transport and on breathing fine mountain air again, and on the fact that they were on horseback. They agreed it was impossible to appreciate that we were really at war— that we were in the enemy's country. We had been riding in this pleasant fashion for an hour and a half with brief halts for rest, when Wood stopped the head of the column, and rode down the trail to meet Capron, who was coming back. Wood returned immediately, leading his horse, and said to Roosevelt:

"Pass the word back to keep silence in the ranks."

The place at which we had halted was where the trail narrowed, and proceeded sharply downward. There was on one side of it a stout barbed-wire fence of five strands. By some fortunate accident this fence had been cut just where the head of the column halted. On the left of the trail it shut off fields of high grass blocked at every fifty yards with great barricades of undergrowth and tangled trees and chapparal. On the other side of the trail there was not a foot of free ground; the bushes seemed absolutely impenetrable, as indeed they were later found to be.

When we halted the men sat down beside the trail and chewed the long blades of grass, or fanned the air with their hats. They had no knowledge of the situation such as their leaders possessed, and their only emotion was one of satisfaction at the chance the halt gave them to rest and to shift their packs. Wood again walked down the trail with Capron and disappeared, and one of the officers informed us that the scouts had seen the outposts of the enemy. It did not seem reasonable that the Spaniards, who had failed to attack us when we landed at Baiquiri, would oppose us until they could do so in force, so, personally, I doubted that there were any Spaniards nearer than Santiago. But we tied our horses to the wire fence, and Capron's troop knelt with carbines at the "ready," peering into the bushes. We must have waited there, while Wood reconnoitred, for over ten minutes. Then he returned, and began deploying his troops out at either side of the trail. Capron he sent on down the trail itself. G Troop was ordered to beat into the bushes on the right, and K and A were sent over the ridge on which we stood down into the hollow to connect with General Young's column on the opposite side of the valley. F and E Troops were deployed out in skirmish-line on the other side of the wire fence. Wood had discovered the enemy a few hundred yards from where he expected to find him, and so far from being "surprised," he had time, as I have just described, to get five of his troops into position before a shot was fired. The firing, when it came, started suddenly on our right. It

THE GUASIMAS FIGHT

sounded so close that—still believing we were acting on a false alarm, and that there were no Spaniards ahead of us—I guessed it was Capron's men firing at random to disclose the enemy's position. I ran after G Troop under Captain Llewellyn, and found them breaking their way

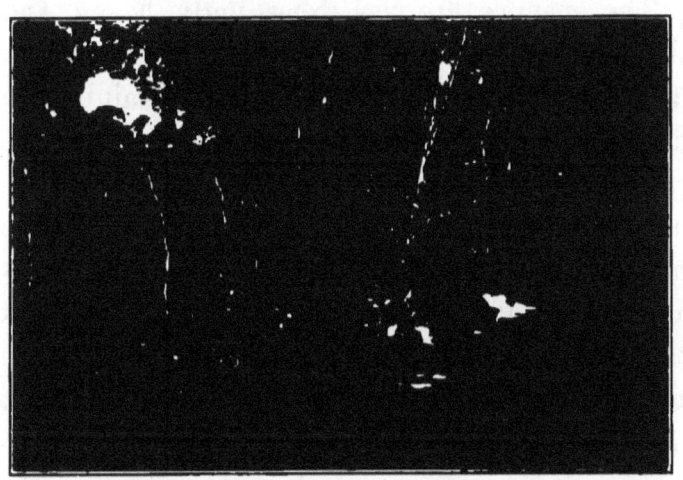

The Place Where the Guasimas Fight Began.

through the bushes in the direction from which the volleys came. It was like forcing the walls of a maze. If each trooper had not kept in touch with the man on either hand he would have been lost in the thicket. At one moment the underbrush seemed swarming with troopers, and the next, except that you heard the twigs breaking, and the heavy breathing of the men, or a crash as a vine pulled someone down, there was not a sign of a human being anywhere. In a few minutes they all broke through into a little open place in front of a dark curtain of vines, and the men fell on one knee and began returning the fire that came from it.

The enemy's fire was exceedingly heavy, and the aim was low. Whether the Spaniards saw us or not we could not tell; we certainly saw nothing of the Spaniards, except a few on the ridge across the valley. The fire against us was not more than fifty to eighty yards away, and so hot that our men could only lie flat in the grass and fire in that position. It was at this moment that the men believed they were being fired on by Capron's troop, which they imagined must have swung to the right, and having lost its bearings and hearing them advancing through the underbrush, had mistaken them for the enemy. They accordingly ceased firing and began shouting in order to warn Capron that he was shooting at his friends. This is the foundation for the statement which was frequently made that the Rough Riders had fired on each other, which they did not do then or at any other time. Later we examined the relative position of the trail which Capron held, and the position of G Troop, and they were at right angles to one another. Capron could not possibly have fired into us at any time, unless he had turned directly around in his tracks and aimed up the very trail he had just descended. Advancing, he could no more have hit us than he could have seen us out of the back of his head. When we found many hundred spent cartridges of the Spaniards a hundred yards in front of G Troop's position, the question as to who did the firing was answered.

It was an exceedingly hot corner. The whole troop was gathered in the little open place blocked by the network of grape-vines and tangled bushes before it. They could not see twenty feet on three sides of them, but on the right hand lay the valley, and across it came the sound of Young's brigade, who were apparently heavily engaged. The enemy's fire was so close that the men could not hear the word of command, and Captain Llewellyn, by word of voice, and Lieutenant Greenway, unable to get their attention, ran among them, batting them with their sombreros to make them cease firing. Lieutenant-Colonel Roosevelt ran up just then, bringing with him Lieutenant Woodbury Kane and ten troopers from K Troop. Roosevelt lay down in the grass beside Llewellyn and consulted with him eagerly.

Kane was smiling with the charming content of a perfectly happy man, exactly as though it were a polo match and his side had scored. When Captain Llewellyn told him his men were not needed, and to rejoin his troop, he led his detail over the edge of the hill on which we lay, although the bullets were passing three feet high. As he disappeared below the crest, walking quite erect, he was still smiling. Roosevelt pointed out that it was impossible to advance farther on account of the network of wild grape-vines that masked the Spaniards from us, and that we must cross the trail and make to the left. The shouts the men had raised to warn Capron had established our position to the enemy, and the firing was now fearfully accurate. Sergeant Russell, who in his day had been a colonel on a governor's staff, was killed, and the other sergeant was shot through the wrist. In the space of three minutes nine men were lying on their backs helpless. The men drew off slowly to the left, dragging the wounded with them. Owing to the low aim of the enemy, they were forced to move on their knees and crawl on their stomachs. Even then they were hit. One man near me was shot through the head. Returning two hours later to locate the body, I found that the buzzards had

THE GUASIMAS FIGHT

torn off his lips and his eyes. This mutilation by these hideous birds is, no doubt, what Admiral Sampson mistook for the work of the Spaniards, when the bodies of the marines at Guantanamo were found disfigured in the same fashion. K Troop had meantime deployed into the valley

Siboney, from the Hill Over which the Wounded Rough Riders Retired After the Fight.

under the fire from the enemy on the ridge. It had been ordered to establish communication with General Young's column, and while advancing and firing on the ridge, Captain Jenkins sent the guidon-bearer back to climb the hill and wave his red and white banner where Young's men could see it. The guidon-bearer had once run for Congress on the gold ticket in Arizona, and, as someone said, was naturally the man who should have been selected for a forlorn hope. His flag brought him instantly under a heavy fire, but he continued waving it until the Tenth Cavalry on the other side of the valley answered, and the two columns were connected by a skirmish-line composed of K Troop and A, under Captain "Bucky" O'Neill.

G Troop meanwhile had hurried over to the left, and passing through the opening in the wire-fence had spread out into open order. It followed down after Captain Luna's troop and D and E Troops, which were well already in advance. Roosevelt ran forward and took command of the extreme left of this line. Wood was walking up and down along it, leading his horse, which he thought might be of use in case he had to move quickly to alter his original formation—at present his plan was to spread out his men so that they would join Young on the right, and on the left swing around until they flanked the enemy. K and A Troops had already succeeded in joining hands with Young's column across the valley, and as they were capable of taking care of themselves, Wood was bending his efforts to keep his remaining four companies in

THE GUASIMAS FIGHT

a straight line and revolving them around the enemy's "end." It was in no way an easy thing to do. The men were at times wholly hidden from each other, and from him; probably at no one time did he see more than two of his troops together. It was only by the firing that he could tell where his men lay, and that they were always steadily advancing.

The advances were made in quick, desperate rushes—sometimes the ground gained was no more than a man covers in sliding for a base. At other times half a troop would rise and race forward and then burrow deep in the hot grass and fire. On this side of the line there was an occasional glimpse of the enemy. But for a great part of the time the men shot at the places from where the enemy's fire seemed to come, aiming low and answering in steady volleys. The fire discipline was excellent. The prophets of evil of the Tampa Bay Hotel had foretold that the cowboys would shoot as they chose, and, in the field, would act independently of their officers. As it turned out, the cowboys were the very men who waited most patiently for the officers to give the word of command. At all times the movement was without rest, breathless and fierce, like a cane-rush, or a street-fight.

After the first three minutes every man had stripped as though for a wrestling-match, throwing off all his impedimenta but his cartridge-belt and canteen. Even then the sun handicapped their strength cruelly. The enemy were hidden in the shade of the jungle, while they had to fight in the open for every thicket they gained, crawling through grass which was as hot as a steam bath, and with their flesh and clothing torn by thorns and the sword-like blade of the Spanish "bayonet." The glare of the sun was full in their eyes and as fierce as a limelight.

When G Troop passed on across the trail to the left I stopped at the place where the column had first halted—it had been converted into a dressing station and the wounded of G troop were left there in the care of the hospital stewards. A tall, gaunt young man with a cross on his arm was just coming back up the trail. His head was bent, and by some surgeon's trick he was advancing rapidly with great strides, and at the same time carrying a wounded man much heavier than himself across his shoulders. As I stepped out of the trail he raised his head, and smiled and nodded, and left me wondering where I had seen him before, smiling in the same cheery, confident way and moving in that same position. I knew it could not have been under the same conditions, and yet he was certainly associated with another time of excitement and rush and heat, and then I remembered him. He had been covered with blood and dirt and perspiration as he was now, only then he wore a canvas jacket and the man he carried on his shoulders was trying to hold him back from a white-washed line. And I recognized the young doctor with the blood bathing his breeches as "Bob" Church, of Princeton. That was only one of four badly wounded men he carried on his shoulders that day over a half-mile of trail that stretched from the firing-line back to the dressing station under an unceasing fire. And as the senior surgeon was absent he had chief responsibility that day for all the wounded, and that so few of them died is greatly due to this young man who went down into the firing-line and pulled them from it, and bore them out of danger. Some of the comic paragraphers who wrote of the members of the Knickerbocker Club and the college swells of the Rough Riders organization, and of their imaginary valets and golf clubs, ought, in decency, since the fight at Guasimas to go out and hang themselves with remorse. For the same spirit that once sent these men down a white-washed field against their opponents' rush-line was the spirit that sent Church, Channing, Devereux, Ronalds, Wrenn, Cash, Bull, Larned, Goodrich, Greenway, Dudley Dean, and

Sergeant Tiffany. Lt. Woodbury Kane. Major Dunn. Captain Jenkins. Lt. H. K. Devereux.

A Group of Rough Riders.

a dozen others through the high hot grass at Guasimas, not shouting, as their friends the cowboys did, but each with his mouth tightly shut, with his eyes on the ball, and moving in obedience to

THE GUASIMAS FIGHT

the captain's signals. Judging from the sound, our firing-line now seemed to be half a mile in advance of the place where the head of the column had first halted. This showed that the Spaniards had been driven back at least three hundred yards from their original position. It was impossible to see any of our men in the field, so I ran down the trail with the idea that it would lead me back to the troop I had left when I had stopped at the dressing station. The walk down that trail presented one of the most grewsome and saddest pictures of the war. It narrowed as it descended; it was for that reason the enemy had selected that part of it for the attack, and the vines and bushes interlaced so closely above it that the sun could not come through.

The rocks on either side were spattered with blood and the rank grass was matted with it. Blanket-rolls, haversacks, carbines, and canteens had been abandoned all along its length, so that the trail looked as though a retreating army had fled along it, rather than that one company had fought its way through it to the front. Except for the clatter of the land-crabs, those hideous orchid-colored monsters that haunt the places of the dead, and the whistling of the bullets in the trees, the place was as silent as a grave. For the wounded lying along its length were as still as the dead beside them. The noise of the loose stones rolling under my feet brought a hospital steward out of the brush, and he called after me:

"Lieutenant Thomas is badly wounded in here, and we can't move him. We want to carry him out of the sun some place, where there is shade and a breeze." Thomas was the first lieutenant of Capron's troop. He is a young man, large and powerfully built. He was shot through the leg just below the trunk, and I found him lying on a blanket half naked and covered with blood, and with his leg bound in tourniquets made of twigs and pocket-handkerchiefs. It gave one a thrill of awe and wonder to see how these cowboy-surgeons, with a stick that one would use to light a pipe and with the gaudy 'kerchiefs they had taken from their necks, were holding death at bay. The young officer was in great pain and tossing and raving wildly. When we gathered up the corners of his blanket and lifted him, he tried to sit upright, and cried out, "You're taking me to the front, aren't you? You said you would. They've killed my captain—do you understand? They've killed Captain Capron. The ——— Mexicans! They've killed my captain."

The troopers assured him they were carrying

him to the firing-line, but he was not satisfied. We stumbled over the stones and vines, bumping his wounded body against the ground and leaving a black streak in the grass behind us, but it seemed to hurt us, more than it did him, for he sat up again seizing the men by the wrists imploringly with his bloody hands.

"For God's sake, take me to the front," he begged. "Do you hear me, I order you; damn you, I order— We must give them hell; do you hear? we must give them hell. They've killed Capron. They've killed my captain."

The loss of blood and the heat at last mercifully silenced him, and when we had reached the trail he had fainted and I left them kneeling around him, their grave boyish faces filled with sympathy and concern.

Only fifty feet from him and farther down the trail I passed his captain, with his body propped against Church's knee and with his head fallen on the surgeon's shoulder. Capron was always a handsome, soldierly looking man—some said that he was the most soldierly looking of any of the young officers in the army—and as I saw him then death had given him a great dignity and nobleness. He was only twenty-eight years old, the age when life has just begun, but he rested his head on the surgeon's shoulder like a man who knew he was already through with it and that, though they might peck and mend at the body, he had received his final orders. His breast and shoulders were bare, and as the surgeon cut the tunic from him the sight of his great chest and the skin, as white as a girl's, and the black open wound against it made the yellow stripes and the brass insignia of rank seem strangely mean and tawdry.

Fifty yards farther on, around a turn in the trail, behind a rock, a boy was lying with a bullet-wound between his eyes. His chest was heaving with short, hoarse noises which I guessed were due to some muscular action entirely, and that he was virtually dead. I lifted him and gave him some water, but it would not pass through his fixed teeth. In the pocket of his blouse was a New Testament with the name *Fielder Dawson, Mo.*, scribbled in it in pencil. While I was writing it down for identification, a boy as young as himself came from behind me down the trail.

"It is no use," he said, "the surgeon has seen him; he says he is just the same as dead. He is my bunkie; we only met two weeks ago at San Antonio; but he and me had got to be such good

Wounded Rough Riders Coming Over the Hill at Siboney. Head of Column of Second Infantry Going to Support the Rough Riders, June 24th.

friends— But there's nothing I can do now." He threw himself down on the rock beside his bunkie, who was still breathing with that hoarse inhuman rattle, and I left them, the one who had been spared looking down helplessly with the tears creeping across his cheeks.

The firing was quite close now, and as I continued the trail was no longer filled with blanket-rolls and haversacks, nor did pitiful, prostrate figures lie in wait behind each rock. I guessed this must mean that I was now well in advance of the farthest point to which Capron's troop had moved before it had deployed to the left, and I was running forward feeling confident that I must be close on our men when I saw far in advance the body of a sergeant blocking the trail and stretched at full length across it. Its position was a hundred yards in advance of that of any of the others—it was apparently the body of the first man killed. After death the bodies of some men seem to shrink almost instantly within themselves; they become limp and shapeless, and their uniforms hang upon them strangely. But this man, who was a giant in life, remained a giant in death—his very attitude was one of attack; his fists were clinched, his jaw set, and his eyes, which were still human, seemed fixed with resolve. He was dead, but he was not defeated. And so Sergeant Fish died as he had lived—defiantly, running into the very face of the enemy, standing squarely upright on his legs instead of crouching, as the others called to him to do, until he fell like a column across the trail. "God gives," was the motto on the watch I took from his blouse, and God could not have given him a nobler end; to die, in the forefront of the first fight of the war, quickly, painlessly, with a bullet through the heart, with his regiment behind him, and facing the enemies of his country.

The line at this time was divided by the trail into two wings. The right wing, composed of K and A Troops, was advancing through the valley, returning the fire from the ridge as it did so, and the left wing, which was much the longer of the two, was swinging around on the enemy's right flank, with its own right resting on the barbed-wire fence. I borrowed a carbine from a wounded man, and joined the remnant of L Troop which was close to the trail.

This troop was then commanded by Second Lieutenant Day, who on account of his conduct that morning and at the battle of San Juan later, when he was shot through the arm, was promoted to be captain of L Troop, or, as it is now officially

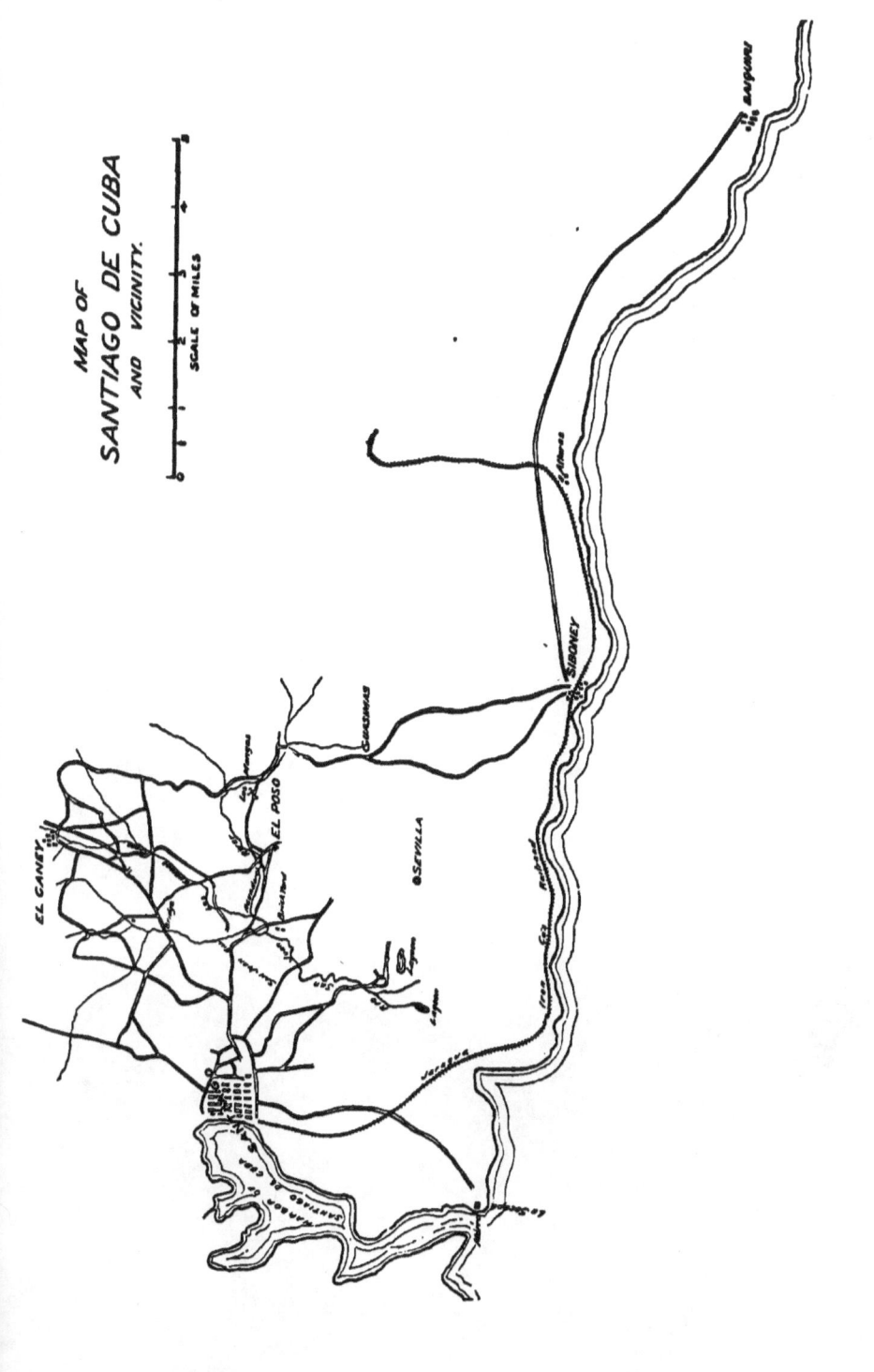

designated, Capron's troop. He was walking up and down the line as unconcernedly as though we were at target-practice, and an English sergeant, Byrne, was assisting him by keeping up a continuous flow of comments and criticisms that showed the keenest enjoyment of the situation. Byrne was the only man I noticed who seemed to regard the fight as in any way humorous. I suspect Byrne was Irish. I saw no one who was in the least alarmed, for at Guasimas no one had time to pose, or to be flippant, or to exhibit any signs of braggadocio. It was for all of them, from the moment it started, through the hot, exhausting hour and a half that it lasted, a most serious proposition. The conditions were exceptional. The men had made a night march the evening before, had been given but three hours troubled sleep on the wet ground, and had then been marched in full equipment up hill and under a cruelly hot sun, right into action. Not one man in the regiment had ever fired a Krag-Jorgensen carbine until he fired it at a Spaniard, for their arms had been issued to them so soon before sailing that they had only drilled with them without using cartridges, and perhaps eighty per cent. of them had never been under fire before. To this handicap was also added the nature of the

THE CUBAN AND PORTO RICAN CAMPAIGNS

ground and the fact that our men could not see their opponents. Their own men fell or rolled over on every side, shot down by an invisible enemy, with no one to retaliate upon in return, with no sign that the attack might not go on indefinitely. Yet they never once took a step backward, but advanced grimly, cleaning a bush or thicket of its occupants before charging it, and securing its cover for themselves, and answering each volley with one that sounded like an echo of the first. The men were panting for breath; the sweat ran so readily into their eyes that they could not see the sights of their guns; then limbs unused to such exertion after seven days of cramped idleness on the troop-ship trembled with weakness and the sun blinded and dazzled them; but time after time they rose and staggered forward through the high grass, or beat their way with their carbines against the tangle of vines and creepers. A mile and a half of territory was gained foot by foot in this brave fashion, the three Spanish positions carried in that distance being marked by the thousands of Mauser cartridges that lay shining and glittering in the grass and behind the barricades of bushes. But this distance had not been gained without many losses, for everyone in the regiment was

THE GUASIMAS FIGHT

engaged. Even those who, on account of the heat had dropped out along the trail, as soon as the sound of the fight reached them, came limping to the front—and plunged into the firing-line. It was the only place they could go—there was no other line. With the exception of Church's dressing station and its wounded there were no reserves.

Among the first to be wounded was the correspondent, Edward Marshall, of the New York *Journal*, who was on the firing-line to the left. He was shot through the body near the spine, and when I saw him he was suffering the most terrible agonies, and passing through a succession of convulsions. He nevertheless, in his brief moments of comparative peace, bore himself with the utmost calm, and was so much a soldier to duty that he continued writing his account of the fight until the fight itself was ended. His courage was the admiration of all the troopers, and he was highly commended by Colonel Wood in the official account of the engagement.

Nothing so well illustrated how desperately each man was needed, and how little was his desire to withdraw, as the fact that the wounded lay where they fell until the hospital stewards found them. Their comrades did not seek that excuse to go to the rear.

The fight had now lasted an hour, and the line had reached a more open country, with a slight incline upward toward a wood, on the edge of which was a ruined house. This house was a former distillery for *aguardiente*, and was now occupied in force by the enemy. Lieutenant-Colonel Roosevelt on the far left was moving up his men with the intention of taking this house on the flank; Wood, who was all over the line, had the same objective point in his mind. The troop commanders had a general idea that the distillery was the key to the enemy's position, and were all working in that direction. It was extremely difficult for Wood and Roosevelt to communicate with the captains, and after the first general orders had been given them they relied upon the latter's intelligence to pull them through. I do not suppose Wood saw more than thirty of his men out of the five hundred engaged at any one time. When he had passed one troop, except for the noise of its volley firing, it was immediately lost to him in the brush, and it was so with the next. Still, so excellent was the intelligence of the officers, and so ready the spirit of the men, that they kept an almost perfect alignment, as was shown when the final order came to charge in the open fields. The advance upon the ruined building was made in stubborn, short rushes, sometimes in silence, and sometimes firing as we ran. The order to fire at will was seldom given, the men waiting patiently for the officers' signal, and then answering in volleys. Some of the men who were twice Day's age begged him to let them take the enemy's impromptu fort on the run, but he answered them tolerantly like spoiled children, and held them down until there was a lull in the enemy's fire, when he would lead them forward, always taking the advance himself. It was easy to tell which men were used to hunting big game in the West and which were not, by the way they made these rushes. The Eastern men broke at the word, and ran for the cover they were directed to take like men trying to get out of the rain, and fell panting on their faces, while the Western trappers and hunters slipped and wriggled through the grass like Indians; dodging from tree-trunk to tree-trunk, and from one bush to another. They always fell into line at the same time with the others, but they had not exposed themselves once while doing so. Some of the escapes were little short of miraculous. The man on my right, Champneys Marshall, of Washington, had one bullet pass through his sleeve, and another pass through his shirt, where it was pulled close to his spine. The holes where the ball entered and went out again were clearly cut. Another man's skin was slightly burned by three bullets in three distinct lines, as though it had been touched for an instant by the lighted end of a cigar. Greenway was shot through his shirt across the breast, and Roosevelt was so close to one bullet, when it struck a tree, that it filled his eyes and ears with tiny splinters. Major Brodie and Lieutenant Thomas were both wounded within a few feet of Colonel Wood, and his color-sergeant, Wright, who followed close at his heels, was clipped three times in the head and neck, and four bullets passed through the folds of the flag he carried. One trooper, Rowland, of Deming, was shot through the lower ribs; he was ordered by Roosevelt to fall back to the dressing station, but there Church told him there was nothing he could do for him then, and directed him to sit down until he could be taken to the hospital at Siboney. Rowland sat still for a short time, and then remarked, restlessly, "I don't seem to be doing much good here," and picking up his carbine, returned to the front. There Roosevelt found him.

"I thought I ordered you to the rear," he demanded.

"Yes, sir, you did," Rowland said, "but there didn't seem to be much doing back there."

He was sent to Siboney with the rest of the wounded, and two days later he appeared in camp. He had marched from Siboney, a distance of six miles, and up hill all the way, carrying his carbine, canteen, and cartridge-belt.

"I thought you were in hospital," Wood said.

"I was," Rowland answered, sheepishly, "but I didn't seem to be doing any good there."

They gave him up as hopeless after that, and he continued his duties and went into the fight of the San Juan hills with the hole still through his ribs. Another cowboy named Heffner, when shot through the body, asked to be propped up against a tree with his canteen and cartridge-belt beside him, and the last his troop saw of him he was seated alone grimly firing over their heads in the direction of the enemy. Church told of another young man shot through the chest. The entrance to his wound was so small that Church could not insert enough of the gauze-packing to stop the flow of blood.

"I'm afraid I'll have to make this hole larger," he said to the boy, "or you'll bleed to death."

"All right," the trooper answered, "I guess

you know best, only you'd better hurry." The boy stretched out on his back and lay perfectly quiet while Church, with a pair of curved scissors, cut away the edges of the wound. His patient neither whimpered nor swore, but stared up at the sun in silence. The bullets were falling on every side of them, and the operation was a hasty one, but the trooper made no comment until Church said, "We'd better get out of this; can you stand being carried?"

"Do you think you can carry me?" the trooper asked.

"Yes."

"Well, I guess you know," the boy answered, holding up his arms.

Another of the Rough Riders was brought to the dressing-station with a shattered ankle, and Church, after bandaging it, gave him his choice of riding down to Siboney on a mule, or of being carried a day later, on a litter.

"If you think you can manage to ride the mule with that broken foot," he said, "you can start at once, but if you wait until to-morrow, when I can spare the men, you can be carried all the way."

The cowboy preferred to start at once, so six hospital stewards lifted him up and dropped him on the mule, and into a huge Mexican saddle. He stuck his wounded ankle into one stirrup, and his untouched one into the other, and gathered up the reins.

"Does it pain you? Do you think you can stand it?" Church asked, anxiously. The cowboy turned and smiled down upon him with supreme disdain.

"What, stand this?" he cried. "Why, this is just like getting money from home."

Toward the last, the firing from the enemy sounded less near, and the bullets passed much higher. Roosevelt, who had picked up a carbine and was firing occasionally to give the direction to the others, determined upon a charge. Wood, at the other end of the line, decided at the same time upon the same manœuvre. It was called "Wood's bluff" afterward, for he had nothing to back it with; while to the enemy it looked as though his whole force was but the skirmish-line in advance of a regiment. The Spaniards naturally could not believe that this thin line which suddenly broke out of the bushes and from behind trees and came cheering out into the hot sunlight in full view, was the entire fighting force against it. They supposed the regiment was coming close on its heels, and as they hate being rushed as a cat hates water, they fired a few parting volleys and broke and ran. The cheering had the same invigorating effect on our own side as a cold shower; it was what first told half the men where the other half were, and it made every individual man feel better. As we knew it was only a bluff, the first cheer was wavering, but the sound of our own voices was so comforting that the second cheer was a howl of triumph. As it was, the Spaniards thought the Rough Riders had already disregarded all the rules of war.

"When we fired a volley," one of the prisoners said later, "instead of falling back they came forward. That is not the way to fight, to come closer at every volley." And so, when instead of retreating on each volley, the Rough Riders rushed at them, cheering and filling the hot air with wild cowboy yells, the dismayed enemy retreated upon Santiago, where he announced he had been attacked by the entire American Army. One of the residents of Santiago asked one of the soldiers if those Americans fought well.

"Well!" he replied, "they tried to catch us with their hands!"

I have not attempted to give any account of General Young's fight on our right, which was

THE GUASIMAS FIGHT

equally desperate, and, owing to the courage of the colored troops of the Tenth in storming a ridge, equally worthy of praise. But it has seemed better not to try and tell of anything I did not see, but to limit myself to the work of the Rough Riders, to whom, after all, the victory was due, as it was owing to Colonel Wood's charge, which took the Spaniards in flank, that General Wheeler and General Young were able to advance, their own stubborn attack in front having failed to dislodge the enemy from his rifle-pits.

According to the statement of the enemy, who had every reason not to exaggerate the size of his own force, 4,000 Spaniards were engaged in this action. The Rough Riders numbered 534, of whom 8 were killed and 34 wounded, and General Young's force numbered 464, of which there were 8 killed and 18 wounded. The American troops accordingly attacked a force over four times their own number intrenched behind rifle-pits and bushes in a mountain-pass. In spite of the smokeless powder used by the Spaniards, which hid their position, the Rough Riders routed them out of it, and drove them back from three different barricades until they made their last stand in the ruined distillery, whence they finally drove them by assault. The eager spirit in which all was done is best described in the Spanish soldier's answer to the inquiring civilian, "They tried to catch us with their hands." It should be the Rough Riders' motto.

CHAPTER VI

THE BATTLE OF SAN JUAN

AFTER the Guasimas fight on June 24th, at Guasimas, the army was advanced along the single trail which leads from Siboney on the coast to Santiago. Two streams of excellent water run parallel with this trail for short distances, and some eight miles from the coast crossed it in two places. Our outposts were stationed at the first of these fords, the Cuban outposts a mile and a half farther on at the ford nearer Santiago, where the stream made a sharp turn at a place called El Poso. Another mile and a half of trail extended from El Poso to the trenches of San Juan. The reader should remember El Poso, as it marked an important starting-point against San Juan on the eventful first of July.

For six days the army was encamped on either side of the trail for three miles back from the outposts. The regimental camps touched each other, and all day long the pack-trains passed up and down between them, carrying the day's rations. The trail was a sunken wagon road, where it was possible, in a few places, for two wagons to pass at one time, but the greater distances were

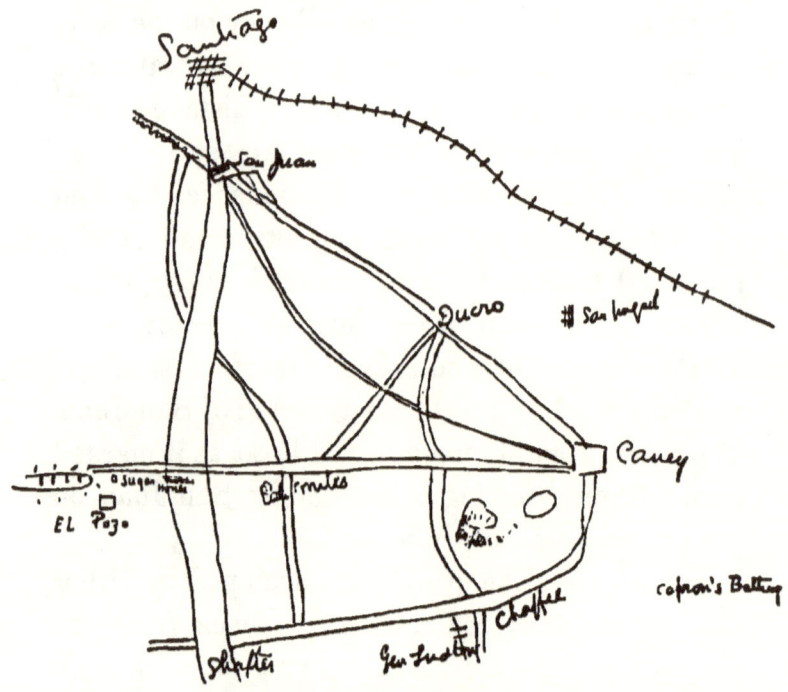

Map of the Country Before San Juan.

This map is reproduced to show how inadequate was the information furnished the commanding generals, concerning the nature of the country before San Juan. It is a copy made by Mr. Davis of the only map issued to General Sumner, the night before the battle. His aides copied this copy and had no other information by which to direct and manœuvre all the regiments of the Cavalry division.

so narrow that there was but just room for a wagon, or a loaded mule-train, to make its way. The banks of the trail were three or four feet high, and when it rained it was converted into a huge gutter, with sides of mud, and with a liquid mud a foot deep between them. The camps were pitched along the trail as near the parallel stream as possible, and in the occasional places where there was rich, high grass. At night the men slept in dog tents, open at the front and back, and during the day spent their time under the shade of trees along the trail, or on the banks of the stream. Sentries were placed at every few feet along these streams to guard them from any possible pollution. For six days the army rested in this way, for as an army moves and acts only on its belly, and as the belly of this army was three miles long, it could advance but slowly.

This week of rest, after the cramped life of the troop-ship, was not ungrateful, although the rations were scarce and there was no tobacco, which was as necessary to the health of the men as their food. Tobacco to many people is a luxury, to men who smoke it is a necessity. The men before Santiago, who were forced to go without their stimulant for four days, suffered just as greatly as a dipsomaniac who is cut off from alcohol. When I said this before in a cable from Santiago, an army officer wrote to some paper and ridiculed the idea, and asked if we were to believe the American soldiers were hysterical, nervous girls.

They are not that, of course, but these men before San Juan actually suffered as much for tobacco as they did for food. With a pipe the soldier can kill hunger, he can forget that he is wet and exhausted and sick with the heat, he can steady his nerves against the roof of bullets when they pass continually overhead, as they did on the 2d of July. After leaving Siboney, the regulars paid two dollars for a plug of tobacco which usually costs them eight cents. Those who could not get tobacco at all smoked dried grass, roots, and dry manure. For several nights the nerves of some of them were so unstrung for the need of the stimulant that they could not sleep. That is a condition of the nerves to be

General Chaffee in the Field.

avoided if possible when men are going into a battle.

The transports carried all the tobacco needed, but in the mind of some commissary officers tobacco is in the class with canned peaches, jellies, and lime-juice, a sort of luxury to be issued after the bacon and coffee and hard-tack have been sent to the front. This should really be considered equally important with the coffee, which the soldier needs three times a day. His tobacco he must have every hour of the day.

But in spite of the lack of tobacco and food, the six days ashore were interesting and busy. The men scoured the woods and hills for mangoes and cocoa-nuts and loafed in the shade beside the beautiful streams, and their officers reconnoitred the hills above them. But I cannot find out that anyone reconnoitred the wooded basin which lies before San Juan. I know a man who says he knows another man who told him he did so, but of thorough reconnoissance there was absolutely none. The temper of the young officers was keen for just such adventure, any number of them were eager to scout, to make actual surveys of the trails leading to Santiago, to discover the best cover and the open places, where the fords crossed the streams, and the trails which flanked the Spanish trenches. But their services were not required. Major-General Chaffee seems to have been the only officer who acquainted himself with that mile and a half of unknown country into which, on the 1st of July, the men were driven as cattle are chased into the chutes of the Chicago cattle-pen. His rank permitted him to take such excursions on his own responsibility, but there were hundreds of other officers who would have been glad of a like opportunity, and there were, in the Rough Riders' Regiment alone, several hundred men who for years had been engaged in just that work, scouting and trailing. But the only reconnoissance the officers were permitted to make was to walk out a mile and a half beyond the outposts to the hill of El Poso, and to look across the basin that lay in the great valley which leads to Santiago. The left of the valley was the hills which hide the sea. The right of the valley was the hills in which nestle the village of El Caney. Below El Poso, in the basin, the dense green forest stretched a mile and a half to the hills of San Juan. These hills looked so quiet and sunny and well kept that they reminded one of a New England orchard. There was a blue bungalow on a hill to the right, a red bungalow higher up on the right, and in the centre the block-house of

THE BATTLE OF SAN JUAN

San Juan, which looked like a Chinese pagoda. Three-quarters of a mile behind them, with a dip between, were the long white walls of the hospital and barracks of Santiago, wearing thirteen Red Cross flags, and, as was pointed out to the foreign

The Farm House Below El Poso Hill, where Many of the Rough Riders were Wounded by the Third Spanish Shell.

attachés later, two six-inch guns a hundred yards in advance of the Red Cross flags.

It was so quiet, so fair, and so prosperous looking, that it breathed of peace. It seemed as though one might, without accident, walk in and take dinner at the Venus Restaurant, or loll on the benches in the Plaza, or rock in one of the great bent-wood chairs around the patio of the Don Carlos Club.

But, on the 27th of June, a long, yellow pit opened in the hillside of San Juan, and in it we could see straw sombreros rising and bobbing up and down, and under the shade of the blockhouse, blue-coated Spaniards strolling leisurely about or riding forth on little white ponies to scamper over the hills. Officers of every regiment, *attachés* of foreign countries, correspondents and staff officers, daily reported the fact that the rifle-pits were growing in length and in number, and that in plain sight from the hill of El Poso, the enemy was intrenching himself at San Juan, and at the little village of El Caney to the right, where he was marching through the streets. But no artillery was sent to El Poso hill to drop a shell among the busy men at work among the trenches, or to interrupt the street parades in El Caney. For four days before the American soldiers captured the same rifle-pits at El Caney and San Juan, with a loss of two thousand men, they watched these men diligently preparing for their coming, and wondered why there was no order to embarrass or to end these preparations.

It is not a difficult task to criticise the conduct of a campaign when it is finished, to show how

THE BATTLE OF SAN JUAN

Santiago should have been taken after it has been taken; but long before the army moved there were general officers who saw how the approach on the city should be made, and who did not wait until after the 1st of July to explain what should be avoided.

Stone Breastwork with Palm-leaf Roof at South Side of El Caney.

Five days before the battle of San Juan General Chaffee, in my hearing, explained the whole situation, and told what should be done and foretold what eventually happened if certain things were left undone. It was impossible, he said, for the army, without great loss, to debouch from the two trails which left the woods and opened on the country before the San Juan hills. He suggested then that it would be well to cut trails parallel with the entire front of the wood and hidden by it, and with innumerable little trails leading into the open, so that the whole army could be marched out upon the hills at the same moment.

"Of course, the enemy knows where those two trails leave the wood," he said; "they have their guns trained on the openings. If our men leave the cover and reach the plain from those trails alone they will be piled up so high that they will block the road." This is exactly what happened, except that instead of being led to the sacrifice through both trails the men were sent down only one of them, and the loss was even greater in consequence. This is recorded here because even if the general in command did not know what to do, it is satisfactory to remember that we had other commanders there who did, with less political influence, but with greater military intelligence. It is quite safe to say that there is not the least doubt in the minds of any of the officers of the Fifth Army Corps, that had the attack on Santiago been planned by Generals Chaffee, Kent, or Lawton it would have been conducted as admirably as was the Porto Rican campaign, under Generals Miles, Schwan, Henry, and Wilson, and

THE BATTLE OF SAN JUAN

with the loss of one-fourth the number of men who were sacrificed. General Shafter saw the field of battle only once before the fight took place. That was on June 29th, when he rode out to El Poso hill and surveyed the plain below. He was about the last officer in his army corps to climb that hill and make this survey, and he did not again go even that far to the front until the night after the battle, and he did not see the trenches for days after the battle had taken place. His trip to El Poso, which was three miles distant from his head-quarters, was apparently too much for his strength, and the heat during the ride prostrated him so greatly that he was forced to take to his cot, where he spent the greater part of his stay in Cuba before the surrender. On the day after the battle of San Juan he said, hopelessly, to a foreign *attaché*: "I am prostrate in body and mind." He could confess this to a stranger, and yet, so great was the obstinacy, so great the vanity and self-confidence of the man, that, although he held the lives and health of 13,000 soldiers in his care, he did not ask to be relieved of his command. I do not think his not coming to the front was due to personal timidity, although in their anger and exasperation at his absence his officers freely accused him of allowing his personal safety to stand in the way of his duty, and so little regard had they for him that I have heard a colonel countermand his orders in the presence of other

Men of the Twelfth Infantry on the Firing Line at El Caney.

generals. His remaining in the rear was undoubtedly due to physical disability, and to the fact that he was ill and in pain.

There are some people who claim that the very fact of Shafter's retaining command when he was suffering showed his bull-dog pluck and courage, but I cannot accept that point of view. A man who could not survive a ride of three miles on horseback, when his men were tramping many miles on foot with packs and arms, and under a tropical sun; who was so occupied and concerned with a gouty foot that he could not consider a plan of battle, and who sent seven thousand men down a trail he had never seen, should resist the temptation to accept responsibilities his political friends thrust upon him, responsibilities he knows he cannot bear. This is the offence that I impute to Shafter: that while he was not even able to rise and look at the city he had been sent to capture, he still clung to his authority. His self-confidence was untouched. His self-complacency was so great that in spite of blunder after blunder, folly upon folly, and mistake upon mistake, he still believed himself infallible, still bullied his inferior officers, and still cursed from his cot. He quarrelled with Admiral Sampson; he quarrelled with General Garcia; he refused to allow Colonel Greenleaf, Surgeon-in-Chief of the army, to destroy the pest-houses in Siboney, and he disobeyed the two orders sent him by General Miles from Tampa and again from Washington, directing him not to allow our soldiers to occupy the Cuban houses.

The obvious answer which is invariably made to every criticism on General Shafter is that, after all, he was justified in the end, for he did succeed; he was sent to Cuba to take Santiago and he took Santiago. He did not take Santiago. His troops, without the aid they should have received from him of proper reconnoissance and sufficient artillery, devotedly sacrificed themselves and took the hills above Santiago with their bare hands, and it was Admiral Cervera who, in withdrawing his guns which covered the city, made a present of it to the American Army. It must not be forgotten that the departure of Cervera's fleet removed Santiago's chief defence, and the cause of Shafter's coming to Cuba as well. The American people cannot have forgotten Shafter's panic-stricken telegram of July 2d, when he said that our lines were so thin that he feared he might have to withdraw from the position his men had taken. It came like a slap in the face to everyone who believed Santiago was already ours. Nor can they have forgotten that on the very next day Cervera, having preferred to take a desperate chance to save his fleet, rather than remain on guard before the city, and having withdrawn, Shafter no longer cabled of retreat, but demanded surrender.

THE BATTLE OF SAN JUAN

Shafter's demand for surrender was sent in on the morning of the 3d, Cervera did not leave until the afternoon, so the admirers of Shafter

Brigadier-General Sumner who Commanded the Cavalry Division at the Battle of San Juan.

claim that Cervera would not have left the harbor at all if Shafter had not arrived and captured the hills above the city. The truth, however, is that it was not on account of Shafter, but in spite of Shafter, that the hills were taken. I now shall

THE CUBAN AND PORTO RICAN CAMPAIGNS

try to make clear how his plan of attacking the city not only failed, but, before it was abandoned, caused needless loss of life; how it finally was disregarded by the generals at the front, and how the battle was won without him, for he did not see the battle of San Juan, nor direct the battle of San Juan, nor was he consulted by those who did.

On the afternoon of June 30th, Captain Mills rode up to the tent of Colonel Wood, and told him that on account of illness, General Wheeler and General Young had relinquished their commands, and that General Sumner would take charge of the Cavalry Division; that he, Colonel Wood, would take command of General Young's brigade, and Colonel Carroll, of General Sumner's brigade.

"You will break camp and move forward at four o'clock," he said. It was then three o'clock, and apparently the order to move forward at four had been given to each regiment at nearly the same time, for they all struck their tents and stepped down into the trail together. It was as though fifteen regiments were encamped along the sidewalks of Fifth Avenue and were all ordered at the same moment to move into it and march down town. If Fifth Avenue were ten feet wide, one can imagine the confusion.

THE BATTLE OF SAN JUAN

General Chaffee was at General Lawton's headquarters, and they stood apart whispering together about the march they were to take to El Caney. Just over their heads the balloon was ascending for the first time and its great glisten-

The War Balloon Making its First Ascension, on the Day Before the Battle of San Juan.

ing bulk hung just above the tree-tops, and the men in the different regiments, picking their way along the trail, gazed up at it open-mouthed. The head-quarters camp was crowded. After a week of inaction the army, at a moment's notice, was moving forward, and everyone had ridden in haste to learn why.

There were *attachés*, in strange uniforms, self-important Cuban generals, officers from the flagship *New York*, and an army of photographers. At the side of the camp, double lines of soldiers passed slowly along the two paths of the muddy road, while, between them, aides dashed up and down, splashing them with dirty water, and shouting, "You will come up at once, sir." "You will not attempt to enter the trail yet, sir." "General Sumner's compliments, and why are you not in your place?"

Twelve thousand men, with their eyes fixed on a balloon, and treading on each other's heels in three inches of mud, move slowly, and after three hours, it seemed as though every man in the United States was under arms and stumbling and slipping down that trail. The lines passed until the moon rose. They seemed endless, interminable; there were cavalry mounted and dismounted, artillery with cracking whips and cursing drivers, Rough Riders in brown, and regulars, both black and white, in blue. Midnight came, and they were still slipping forward.

General Sumner's head-quarters tent was pitched to the right of El Poso hill. Below us lay the basin a mile and a half in length, and a mile and a half wide, from which a white mist was rising.

Capron's Battery in Action at El Caney.

THE BATTLE OF SAN JUAN

Near us, drowned under the mist, seven thousand men were sleeping, and, farther to the right, General Chaffee's five thousand were lying under the bushes along the trails to El Caney, waiting to march on it and eat it up before breakfast.

The place hardly needs a map to explain it. The trails were like a pitchfork, with its prongs touching the hills of San Juan. The long handle of the pitchfork was the trail over which we had just come, the joining of the handle and the prongs were El Poso. El Caney lay half way along the right prong, the left one was the trail down which, in the morning, the troops were to be hurled upon San Juan. It was as yet an utterly undiscovered country. Three miles away, across the basin of mist, we could see the street-lamps of Santiago shining over the San Juan hills. Above us, the tropical moon hung white and clear in the dark purple sky, pierced with millions of white stars. As we turned in, there was just a little something in the air which made saying "good-night" a gentle farce, for no one went to sleep immediately, but lay looking up at the stars, and after a long silence, and much restless turning on the blanket which we shared together, the second lieutenant said: "So, if anything happens to me, to-morrow, you'll see she gets them, won't you?" Before the moon rose again, every sixth man who had slept in the mist that night was either killed or wounded; but the second lieutenant was sitting on the edge of a Spanish rifle-pit, dirty, sweaty, and weak for food, but victorious, and the unknown she did not get them.

El Caney had not yet thrown off her blanket of mist before Capron's battery opened on it from a ridge two miles in the rear. The plan for the day was that El Caney should fall in an hour. The plan for the day is interesting chiefly because it is so different from what happened. According to the plan the army was to advance in two divisions, along the two trails. Incidentally, General Lawton's division was to pick up El Caney, and when El Caney was eliminated, his division was to continue forward and join hands on the right with the divisions of General Sumner and General Kent. The army was then to rest for that night in the woods, half a mile from San Juan.

On the following morning it was to attack San Juan on the two flanks, under cover of artillery. The objection to this plan, which did not apparently suggest itself to General Shafter, was that an army of twelve thousand men, sleeping within five hundred yards of the enemy's rifle-pits might not unreasonably be expected to pass a bad night. We discovered the next day that not only the five hundred yards but the whole basin was covered by the fire from the rifle-pits. The army could not remain in the woods even by daylight

Gun No. 1 of Grimes's Battery, the First Gun Fired at San Juan Block-House, July 1st.

when it was possible to seek some slight shelter, but according to the plan it was expected to bivouac for the night in these woods, and in the morning to manœuvre and deploy and march through them out to the two flanks of San Juan. How the enemy was to be hypnotized while this was going forward it is difficult to explain.

According to this programme, Capron's battery opened on El Caney and Grimes's battery opened on the pagoda-like block-house of San Juan. The range from El Poso was exactly 2,400 yards, and the firing, as was discovered later, was not very effective. The battery used black powder, and, as a result, after each explosion the curtain of smoke hung over the gun for fully a minute before the gunners could see the San Juan trenches, which was chiefly important because for a full minute it gave a mark to the enemy. The hill on which the battery stood was like a sugar-loaf. Behind it was the farm-house of El Poso, the only building in sight within a radius of a mile, and in it were Cuban soldiers and other non-combatants. The Rough Riders had been ordered to halt in the yard of the farm-house and the artillery horses were drawn up in it, under the lee of the hill. The First and Tenth dismounted Cavalry were encamped a hundred yards from the battery along the ridge. Later I took pains to find out by whose order these troops were placed within such close proximity to a battery, and was informed, by the general in command of the division, that his men had been put in that exact spot by the order of the Commanding General. They might as sensibly have

Artillery Coming Up El Poso Hill.

been ordered to paint the rings in a target while a company was firing at the bull's eye. For the first twenty shots the enemy made no reply, when they did it was impossible, owing to their using smokeless powder, to locate their guns. The third shell fell in among the Cubans in the block-house and among the Rough Riders and the men of the First and Tenth Cavalry, killing some and wounding many. These casualties were utterly unnecessary and were due to the stupidity of whoever placed the men within fifty yards of guns in action. Until after the trenches of San Juan were taken by the infantry the artillery's part in the attack on Santiago was of little value. The hills of San Juan and the fort at El Caney were finally taken by assault and with but little aid from the heavier arm. There were only sixteen three-inch guns with this expedition, which set forth with the known purpose of besieging a city. Military experts say that the sixty guns left behind in Tampa would have been few enough for the work they had to do. It was like going to a fire with a hook and ladder company and leaving the hose and the steam-engines in the engine-house. If the guns which were left at Tampa, and the siege-guns which were left on the transports at Baiquiri had first played on the San Juan hills, and put out the fire there, so many men of the hook and ladder contingent would not have been sacrificed.

A quarter of an hour after the firing began from El Poso one of General Shafter's aides directed General Sumner to advance with his divis-

El Poso, Immediately After the Spanish Fire Ceased. A shell entered, killing Cubans inside.

ion down the Santiago trail, and to halt at the edge of the woods.

"What am I to do then?" asked General Sumner.

"You are to await further orders," the aide answered.

As a matter of fact and history this was prob-

Grimes's Battery at El Poso.

The third Spanish shell fell in among the Cubans in the block-house and among the Rough Riders.

THE BATTLE OF SAN JUAN

ably the last order General Sumner received from General Shafter, until the troops of his division had taken the San Juan hills, as it became impossible to get word to General Shafter, the trail leading to his head-quarters tent, three miles in the rear, being blocked by the soldiers of the First and Tenth dismounted Cavalry, and later, by Lawton's division. General Sumner led the Sixth, Third, and Ninth Cavalry, and the Rough Riders down the trail, with instructions for the First and Tenth to follow. The trail, virgin as yet from the foot of an American soldier, was as wide as its narrowest part, which was some ten feet across. At places it was as wide as Broadway, but only for such short distances that it was necessary for the men to advance in column, in double file. A maze of underbrush and trees on either side was all but impenetrable, and when the officers and men had once assembled into the basin, they could only guess as to what lay before them, or on either flank. At the end of a mile the country became more open, and General Sumner saw the Spaniards intrenched a half mile away on the sloping hills. A stream, called the San Juan River, ran across the trail at this point, and another stream crossed it again two hundred yards farther on. The troops were halted at this first stream, some crossing it, and others deploying in single file to the right. Some were on the banks of the stream, others at the edge of the woods in the bushes. Others lay in the high grass which was so high that it stopped the wind, and so hot that it almost choked and suffocated those who lay in it.

The enemy saw the advance and began firing with pitiless accuracy into the jammed and crowded trail, and along the whole border of the woods. There was not a single yard of ground for a mile to the rear, which was not inside the zone of fire. Our men were ordered not to return the fire but to lie still and wait for further orders. Some of them could see the rifle-pits of the enemy quite clearly and the men in them, but many saw nothing but the bushes under which they lay, and the high grass which seemed to burn when they pressed against it. It was during this period of waiting that the greater number of our men were killed. For one hour they lay on their rifles staring at the waving green stuff around them, while the bullets drove past incessantly, with savage insistence, cutting the grass again and again in hundreds of fresh places. Men in line sprang from the ground and sank back again with a groan, or rolled to one side clinging silently to an

Fording a Stream on the Way to the Front.

THE BATTLE OF SAN JUAN

arm or shoulder. Behind the lines hospital stewards passed continually, drawing the wounded back to the streams, where they laid them in long rows, their feet touching the water's edge and their bodies supported by the muddy bank. Up and down the lines, and through the fords of the

Mule Train Carrying Ammunition from Siboney to San Juan.

streams, mounted aides drove their horses at a gallop, as conspicuous a target as the steeple on a church, and one after another paid the price of his position and fell from his horse wounded or dead. Captain Mills fell as he was giving an order, shot through the forehead behind both eyes; Captain O'Neill of the Rough Riders, as he said, "There is no Spanish bullet made that can kill me." Steel, Swift, Henry, each of them was shot out of his saddle.

Hidden in the trees above the streams, and above the trail, sharpshooters and guerillas added a fresh terror to the wounded. There was no hiding from them. Their bullets came from every side. Their invisible smoke helped to keep their hiding-places secret, and in the incessant shriek of shrapnel and the spit of the Mausers, it was difficult to locate the reports of their rifles. They spared neither the wounded nor recognized the Red Cross, they killed the surgeons and the stewards carrying the litters, and killed the wounded men on the litters. A guerilla in a tree above us shot one of the Rough Riders in the breast, while I was helping him carry Captain Morton Henry to the dressing-station, the ball passing down through him, and a second shot from the same tree, barely missed Henry as he lay on the ground where we had dropped him. He was already twice wounded and so covered with blood that no one could have mistaken his condition. The surgeons at work along the stream dressed the wounds with one eye cast aloft at the trees. It was not the Mauser bullets they feared, though they passed continuously, but too high to do their patients further harm, but the bullets of the sharpshooters which struck fairly in among them, splashing in the water and scattering the pebbles. The sounds of the two bullets were as different as is the sharp pop of a soda-water bottle from the buzzing of an angry wasp.

For a time it seemed as though every second man was either killed or wounded, one came upon them lying behind the bush, under which they had crawled with some strange idea that it would protect them, or crouched under the bank of the stream, or lying on their stomachs and lapping up the water with the eagerness of thirsty dogs. As to their suffering, the wounded were magnificently silent, they neither complained nor groaned, nor cursed.

"I've got a punctured tire," was their grim answer to inquiries. White men and colored men, veterans and recruits and volunteers, each lay waiting for the battle to begin or to end so that he might be carried away to safety, for the wounded were in as great danger after they were hit as though they were in the firing line, but none questioned nor complained.

I came across Lieutenant Roberts, of the Tenth Cavalry, lying under the roots of a tree beside the stream with three of his colored troopers stretched around him. He was shot through the intestines, and each of the three men with him was shot in the arm or leg. They had been overlooked or forgotten, and we stumbled upon them

General Hospital of the First Division.

only by the accident of losing our way. They had no knowledge as to how the battle was going or where their comrades were, or where the enemy was. At any moment, for all they knew, the Spaniards might break through the bushes about them. It was a most lonely picture, the young lieutenant, half naked, and wet with his own blood, sitting upright beside the empty stream, and his three followers crouching at his feet like three faithful watch-dogs, each wearing his red badge of courage, with his black skin tanned to a haggard gray, and with his eyes fixed patiently on the white lips of his officer. When the white soldiers with me offered to carry him back to the dressing-station, the negroes resented it stiffly. "If the Lieutenant had been able to move, we would have carried him away long ago," said the sergeant, quite overlooking the fact that his arm was shattered.

"Oh, don't bother the surgeons about me," Roberts added, cheerfully. "They must be very busy. I can wait."

As yet, with all these killed and wounded, we had accomplished nothing—except to obey orders—which was to await further orders. The observation balloon hastened the end. It came blundering down the trail, and stopped the advance of the First and Tenth Cavalry, and was sent up directly over the heads of our men to observe what should have been observed a week before by scouts and reconnoitring parties. A balloon, two miles to the rear, and high enough in the air to be out of range of the enemy's fire, may some day prove itself to be of use and value. But a balloon on the advance line, and only fifty feet above the tops of the trees, was merely an invitation to the enemy to kill everything beneath it. And the enemy responded to the invitation. A Spaniard might question if he could hit a man, or a number of men, hidden in the bushes, but had no doubt at all as to his ability to hit a mammoth glistening ball only six hundred yards distant, and so all the trenches fired at it at once, and the men of the First and Tenth, packed together directly behind it, received the full force of the bullets. The men lying directly below it received the shrapnel which was timed to hit it, and which at last, fortunately, did hit it. This was endured for an hour, an hour of such hell of fire and heat, that the heat in itself, had there been no bullets, would have been remembered for its cruelty. Men gasped on their backs, like fishes in the bottom of a boat, their heads burning inside and out, their limbs too heavy to move. They had been rushed here and rushed there wet with sweat and wet with fording the streams, under a sun that would have made moving a fan an effort, and they lay prostrate, gasping at the hot air, with faces aflame, and their tongues sticking out, and their eyes

THE BATTLE OF SAN JUAN

rolling. All through this the volleys from the rifle-pits sputtered and rattled, and the bullets sang continuously like the wind through the rigging in a gale, shrapnel whined and broke, and still no order came from General Shafter.

Captain Howse, of General Sumner's staff, rode down the trail to learn what had delayed the First and Tenth, and was hailed by Colonel Derby, who was just descending from the shattered balloon.

"I saw men up there on those hills," Colonel Derby shouted; "they are firing at our troops." That was part of the information contributed by the balloon. Captain Howse's reply is lost to history.

General Kent's division, which was to have been held in reserve, according to the plan, had been rushed up in the rear of the First and Tenth, and the Tenth had deployed in skirmish order to the right. The trail was now completely blocked by Kent's Division. Lawton's Division, which was to have reinforced on the right, had not appeared, but incessant firing from the direction of El Caney showed that he and Chaffee were fighting mightily. The situation was desperate. Our troops could not retreat, as the trail for two miles behind them was wedged with men. They could not remain where they were for they were being shot to pieces. There was only one thing they could do—go forward and take the San Juan hills by assault. It was as desperate as the situation itself. To charge earthworks held by men with modern rifles, and using modern artillery, until after the earthworks have been shaken by artillery, and to attack them in advance and not in the flanks, are both impossible military propositions. But this campaign had not been conducted according to military rules, and a series of military blunders had brought seven thousand American soldiers into a chute of death, from which there was no escape except by taking the enemy who held it by the throat, and driving him out and beating him down. So the generals of divisions and brigades stepped back and relinquished their command to the regimental officers and the enlisted men.

"We can do nothing more," they virtually said. "There is the enemy."

Colonel Roosevelt, on horseback, broke from the woods behind the line of the Ninth, and finding its men lying in his way, shouted: "If you don't wish to go forward, let my men pass, please." The junior officers of the Ninth, with their ne-

The Fight at the San Juan Block-house, July 1st.

groes, instantly sprang into line with the Rough Riders, and charged at the blue block-house on the right.

I speak of Roosevelt first because, with General Hawkins, who led Kent's Division, notably the Sixth and Sixteenth Regulars, he was, without doubt, the most conspicuous figure in the charge. General Hawkins, with hair as white as snow, and yet far in advance of men thirty years his junior, was so noble a sight that you felt inclined to pray for his safety; on the other hand, Roosevelt, mounted high on horseback, and charging the rifle-pits at a gallop and quite alone, made you feel that you would like to cheer. He wore on his sombrero a blue polka-dot handkerchief, à la Havelock, which, as he advanced, floated out straight behind his head, like a guidon. Afterward, the men of his regiment who followed this flag, adopted a polka-dot handkerchief as the badge of the Rough Riders. These two officers were notably conspicuous in the charge, but no one can claim that any two men, or any one man, was more brave or more daring, or showed greater courage in that slow, stubborn advance than did any of the others. Someone asked one of the officers if he had any difficulty in making his men follow him. "No," he answered, "I had some difficulty in keeping up with them." As one of the Brigade Generals said : "San Juan was won by the regimental officers and men. We had as little to do as the referee at a prize-fight who calls 'time.' We called 'time' and they did the fighting."

I have seen many illustrations and pictures of this charge on the San Juan hills, but none of them seem to show it just as I remember it. In the picture-papers the men are running up hill swiftly and gallantly, in regular formation, rank after rank, with flags flying, their eyes aflame, and their hair streaming, their bayonets fixed, in long, brilliant lines, an invincible, overpowering weight of numbers. Instead of which I think the thing which impressed one the most, when our men started from cover, was that they were so few. It seemed as if someone had made an awful and terrible mistake. One's instinct was to call to them to come back. You felt that someone had blundered and that these few men were blindly following out some madman's mad order. It was not heroic then, it seemed merely terribly pathetic. The pity of it, the folly of such a sacrifice was what held you.

They had no glittering bayonets, they were not massed in regular array. There were a few

THE BATTLE OF SAN JUAN

men in advance, bunched together, and creeping up a steep, sunny hill, the tops of which roared and flashed with flame. The men held their guns

San Juan Block-house, Showing Marks of Shot.

pressed across their breasts and stepped heavily as they climbed. Behind these first few, spreading out like a fan, were single lines of men, slipping and scrambling in the smooth grass, moving forward with difficulty, as though they were wading waist high through water, moving slowly, carefully, with strenuous effort. It was much more wonderful than any swinging charge could have been. They walked to greet death at every step, many of them, as they advanced, sinking suddenly or pitching forward and disappearing in the high grass, but the others waded on, stubbornly, forming a thin blue line that kept creeping higher and higher up the hill. It was as inevitable as the rising tide. It was a miracle of self-sacrifice, a triumph of bull-dog courage, which one watched breathless with wonder. The fire of the Spanish riflemen, who still stuck bravely to their posts, doubled and trebled in fierceness, the crests of the hills crackled and burst in amazed roars, and rippled with waves of tiny flame. But the blue line crept steadily up and on, and then, near the top, the broken fragments gathered together with a sudden burst of speed, the Spaniards appeared for a moment outlined against the sky and poised for instant flight, fired a last volley and fled before the swift-moving wave that leaped and sprang up after them.

The men of the Ninth and the Rough Riders rushed to the block-house together, the men of the Sixth, of the Third, of the Tenth Cavalry, of the Sixth and Sixteenth Infantry, fell on their faces

The San Juan Hill, Showing General Wheeler's Camp.

along the crest of the hills beyond, and opened upon the vanishing enemy. They drove the yellow silk flags of the cavalry and the Stars and Stripes of their country into the soft earth of the trenches, and then sank down and looked back at the road they had climbed and swung their hats in the air. And from far overhead, from these few figures perched on the Spanish rifle-pits, with their flags planted among the empty cartridges of the enemy, and overlooking the walls of Santiago, came, faintly, the sound of a tired, broken cheer.

CHAPTER VII

IN THE RIFLE-PITS

THE position of the regulars immediately after they had taken the San Juan hills was painfully suggestive of Humpty-Dumpty on the wall. They did not suggest Humpty-Dumpty at the time, but now one sees that their attitude then was quite as precarious as his and almost as absurd.

Along the top of each hill were tiny groups of not more than from a dozen to fifteen soldiers. They were sprawling on their backs, panting for breath, or sitting with their elbows on their knees and panting for breath. By some miracle they had arrived at this supreme elevation, and they found themselves suddenly in complete possession of several block-houses and rows and rows of abandoned rifle-pits. Three hundred yards below them, in the valley that stretched between the city of Santiago and the hills on which they crouched, thousands of Spanish rifles were spluttering furiously and shrieking with rage and dis-

United States Troops in the Trenches Before Santiago.

appointment, making the crest of hills behind which our men lay absolutely untenable. At their feet were the sunny slopes up which they had just climbed, and which were still swept by fierce and sudden showers of falling bullets. They could neither retreat nor advance, and they were so few that to one coming up the hill they suggested Sunday groups of workmen picnicking on the hills of a city park. They were so few in number, so utterly inadequate to the extent of hills they had captured and which they were supposed to hold, that their position was like that of a man clinging to a church steeple and unable, without breaking his neck, to slip down on any side; but who still proclaimed to the air about him, "See how I hold this steeple!" Their own point of view and sense of relief and surprise were thus best expressed in the words of Stephen Crane's trooper, who sank upon the crest of the hill, panting, bleeding, and sweating, and cried: "Well, hell, here we are!"

I watched the cavalry take the hills they captured from a place on the trail about three hundred yards behind them, near a ford of the San Juan stream, which was later picturesquely called the Bloody Bend, because so many men were hurt there, and because it was used as a dressing station for the wounded. General Wheeler was seated at this ford at the foot of a great tree, and gathered about him were different members of his staff—his son, and Captain William Astor Chanler, and Captain Hardie, who was, much to his disgust, in command of the General's body-guard, and so could not storm the

Making Observations while Under Heavy Spanish Fire.

hill with his regiment. I told General Wheeler that the cavalry had just reached the top of the hill, and I think from his answer that this was the first information that he had received of the fact that the hills were captured. At the same moment an aide rode up and said, "General Wheeler, we have taken the San Juan blockhouse. It is now possible for you to come up to the front." General Wheeler at once rose and walked on up the three hundred yards of trail to the hill; but about half an hour before he reached it I saw General Sumner riding over the hills with his aides: Captain Howse, Lieutenant Harmon, who was wounded, but who still sat in his saddle, and Lieutenant Andrews of Troop G, Third Cavalry, whose horse had been shot, but who trotted along beside Sumner on foot. I mention this, because in General Shafter's general order congratulating the troops on the victory of San Juan, he gave the entire credit for the work of the cavalry division to General Wheeler, speaking of him as leading the dismounted cavalry at the front. He did not mention General Sumner at all. As a matter of history, General Sumner bore the heat and brunt of the day, and was in command of the cavalry division long after the hills were taken, until about four o'clock, when General Wheeler reassumed command. General Wheeler has won so many laurels in the Civil War, and again in this last war, that he does not need honors which belong to another. General Kent, who was also mentioned in the same general order for the good work of his infantry, was most magnanimous, and at the time of the fight gave the credit of the advance to his brigade commander, General Hawkins. In the minds of the army of the rifle-pits this disclaimer on his part did not so much help General Hawkins, who had distinguished himself before the eyes of all, as it added to the great popularity of General Kent. Later General Shafter corrected his original error, and in his final report states that Sumner, and not Wheeler, commanded the cavalry at the battle of San Juan.

During the days while the armies camped in the rifle-pits it was necessary to pass frequently over the trail from the Bloody Bend to the foot of the hill on which stood the San Juan blockhouse, and I now know that the distance between those two points is not over three hundred yards. But on the morning of the first of July, when Mr. Floyd Campbell, the *Herald* artist, and I followed on the footsteps of the regulars it seemed to stretch for many weary miles. It was so long that morning that at about every fifty feet we found it necessary to sit down and rest. We were generally overcome with fatigue wherever there was a tree. There were few trees large enough for our purpose, and they were all occupied. Everyone had been under fire for five hours; but at no place nor time during the entire war did the fire of the enemy seem so unpleasant as it was that morning along that trail. Bullets passed without giving a moment's respite at several different heights, and while doing so made a most demoralizing amount of noise. They struck the trees overhead, the ground underfoot, and cut holes in the air on every side. Sometimes a shrapnel shell burst and tore the men it hit into ribbons of flesh. Dead horses and the bodies of the regulars lay all along the trail, and no one who was not wounded, or supporting wounded, passed down it from the front. It was interesting to observe the pressure which men put upon their nerves suddenly slip from them, and to see them flying panic-stricken for a tree, or dropping on their knees and sliding along the ground. It showed that a man when he is alone can only bear a certain amount of danger, as he can only stand a certain amount of physical fatigue. You would see a soldier walking along the trail quite boldly for a little way, and then a bullet would come too close to his head, or too many of them would whistle by at the same moment, and his nerves would refuse to support the strain any longer, and he would jump for the bushes and would sit there breathing heavily until he mustered up sufficient will-power to carry him farther on. It was hardest for the wounded who had just fallen during the charge up the hill. They had paid their dues, and felt that they deserved a respite; but the bullets pursued them cruelly all the way down the trail, following them like live things, and driving them as with whips to efforts far beyond their strength. There was one big tree which everyone who was at San Juan will remember, and which stood on the left of the trail just between the two streams. It was the rest-house for many men that morning, and it served them well apparently, for a few days later we counted forty-two bullet holes in its trunk. Two officers who were making maps on little boards which hung from their shoulders like a peddler's tray, made for this tree, and three regulars and Campbell and I joined them. It was as though we were seeking shelter from a storm. One of the regulars was crowded out to one side, and he suddenly rolled over on top of us, crying, "I've got it, I've got it," in such a cheerful tone of delight that we did not believe him, and told him to sit still and not spoil our formation. But he showed us where the bullet had entered his shoulder. We might have been under that tree yet had not General Kent ridden by at a gallop, sitting up very stiff in his saddle and, as it were, looking the bullets straight in the eye.

Looking Toward Santiago from the Trenches of the Colored Troops.

IN THE RIFLE-PITS

He made the group behind the tree feel uncomfortable, so the officers with the drawing-boards and the rest of us scrambled to our feet and went up after them. We found our men lying on their backs along the hills just below the crest. They were still panting after their climb, and were not at that time making any effort to return the fire of the enemy. To have done so would have been inviting death, for bullets from machine guns and Mausers were clipping the crest of the hills unceasingly. During this time the correspondents, as usual, shared whatever danger there was with the soldiers, and while the hills were still swept with the enemy's fire Stephen Crane and John Hare, of *Collier's*, came up them, and later John Fox, of *Harper's*, and James Whigham, the golf champion, who was acting as the correspondent of the Chicago *Tribune*, and Sir Bryan Leighton, a correspondent of the New York *Journal*. These were the only correspondents I saw that far up on that day, although several others who had been in the Caney fight arrived later.

Campbell had an insane sense of duty which forced him to take a photograph of Santiago from the crest of the hill, and I had to go where he did. I obtained a very hurried view of the city, and looked at it only long enough to enable me to say truthfully that I had seen it, but not long enough to enable me to recognize it if I saw it again. The artillery under Major Dillenback had just taken up a position on the crest. It remained in position about three minutes. The men loaded the guns lying on their backs and rising on one elbow to open the breech. When the infantry saw them coming up the hill, lashing their horses and bumping the guns into trees and over rocks, with their red blankets and red guidons flashing in the sun, the sight was so inspiring that the tired men cheered and forgot that as yet the artillery had done but little to aid them. The guns came up the hill so fast that it looked as though we would be in Santiago in a few hours, instead of which within the next three minutes the guns were charging just as fast down the hill again, abandoning the infantry and dismounted cavalry to the Spaniards. It is one of the first rules of tactics, I believe, that artillery must be the last arm of the service to leave the field, as the moral effect of its withdrawal upon the infantry is naturally demoralizing. It can be said for the artillery, that it was an absurd proposition to send it to the crest of the hill, where it was exposed to modern rifle-fire at very short range; but still it might have withdrawn in better order.

To reach the crest of the hill I had to pass through a company of infantry which had been sent up in skirmish order to support the artillery during the three minutes in which it was engaged. These men were lying on their faces about fifty feet below the crest, and as I passed among them on my way back I noticed that they wore in their hats the silver badge of the Seventy-first New York and I supposed the regiment below in the block-house from which I had just seen these men detached was the remainder of the Seventy-first. In my despatch to the *Herald*, which I wrote immediately, I mentioned the fact that the Seventy-first was at that writing holding the crest of the San Juan hill. In this I was mistaken, for the company I had seen, with one other, were the only companies of the regiment that took part in the charge. I believe the one on the hill was Company F, under the command of Captain Rafferty. When the newspapers arrived from New York, it appeared from their accounts of the battle that the hills of San Juan had been taken by the Rough Riders and the Seventy-first New York. One paper even said, "Inspired by the example of the Rough

Riders, the Sixth and Ninth Regulars charged the hill with undaunted courage." This injudicious praise was as distasteful to the Rough Riders as it was unfair to the regulars. The Rough Riders were no better than the regulars, although they behaved just as well; but when Colonel Roosevelt, in his letter to the Secretary of War, boasted that they were five times as good as any other regiment of volunteers, he was in my opinion far too modest. They were many times as good as any other volunteer regiment that I ever saw in action and out of action, which is also the same as saying that any regiment of regulars is many times better than any regiment of volunteers. The inside story of the Seventy-first New York is well known to everyone who was present at the fight. The regiment did not run away, but it certainly did not behave well. The fault was entirely that of some of the officers. They funked the fight and, as General Kent describes in his report, refused to leave the bushes, and as a result the men either funked it too, or, as was the case with a dozen from each company, fell in with the regulars of Kent's division, and so reached the crest of the hill with them and led by their officers. It was the first time these volunteers had been under fire, and the fact that

A Detachment of the Seventy-first New York Volunteers just Before Going into Action.

they at first hung back is chiefly interesting because their doing so was another argument against the use of amateurs in time of war. The fulsome praise given to this regiment was a most serious injustice to the men of the regular army who on that day did their full duty, which these volunteers did not. It also strengthens the hands of those politicians who support for their own ends that national menace called the National Guard, and those militia officers who forced their Congressmen to defeat the Hull bill. The militia Colonel can now point to the "gallant Seventy-first" as an example of the bravery and of the value of volunteers in action, when what the country needs to know now is that in actual warfare the volunteer is a nuisance, that it always takes one regular to offset his mistakes, to help him cook his rations, and to teach him to shelter himself and to keep himself clean. The only correspondent who thought it wise to tell the truth concerning the officers of the Seventy-first at the time of the fight was the correspondent of the *World;* but as soon as his paper learned that the truth was not what the friends of the Seventy-first desired, it gave them what they desired, and stultified itself by saying that its correspondent had lied. There is one story which was told in the trenches and which illustrates the feeling that existed there toward the officers of this volunteer

Digging Trenches Before Santiago, about July 10, 1898.

regiment. One of these men was lying hidden in the grass when the order was given to charge the hills. An officer of the regular army in running forward did not see him, and stepped with his heel in the small of the other man's back. The indignant volunteer yelled after him, "Where in hell are you going?"

"To the front," the regular replied, cheerfully. "Where in hell are you going?"

IN THE RIFLE-PITS

After the withdrawal of the artillery General Wheeler came up and established his headquarters at the turn of the trail, in a cut between two of the hills. He remained there, and never left the rifle-pits until Santiago fell.

It was now about four o'clock in the afternoon, and our men were by this time greatly in need of food, and especially of water, for a battle is

Generals Wheeler, Chaffee, and Lawton in Consultation.

the most thirst-creating of all experiences. There was, however, no food of any sort, and the water could only be secured at great risk to the men who left the shelter of the hills to go after it. About the same hour the ammunition wagons came up and halted above General Wheeler's head-quarters, and men from the hills were sent to bring back cartridges. The colored regulars of the Tenth were the first to come down after the ammunition, and seemed overjoyed at the fact that the wagons held cartridges and not, as some supposed, rations. The web belts of most of them were empty, and in no one belt were there more than half-a-dozen or ten of the one hundred and fifty cartridges with which the men had begun the day. The negro soldiers established themselves as fighting men that morning, and the chuckles they gave as they shoved the cartridges into their belts showed that, though they did not have food or water, so long as they had ammunition they were content. About 5 o'clock the Spaniards rallied and poured in a furious fire, which it is now believed was intended to cover the retreat of a large number of their comrades in the direction of Santiago. When the sun sank that night the situation was not encouraging. The enemy was still firing with unabated enthusiasm, and our men were returning his fire with equal desperation. They were still scattered far apart along the hills. They

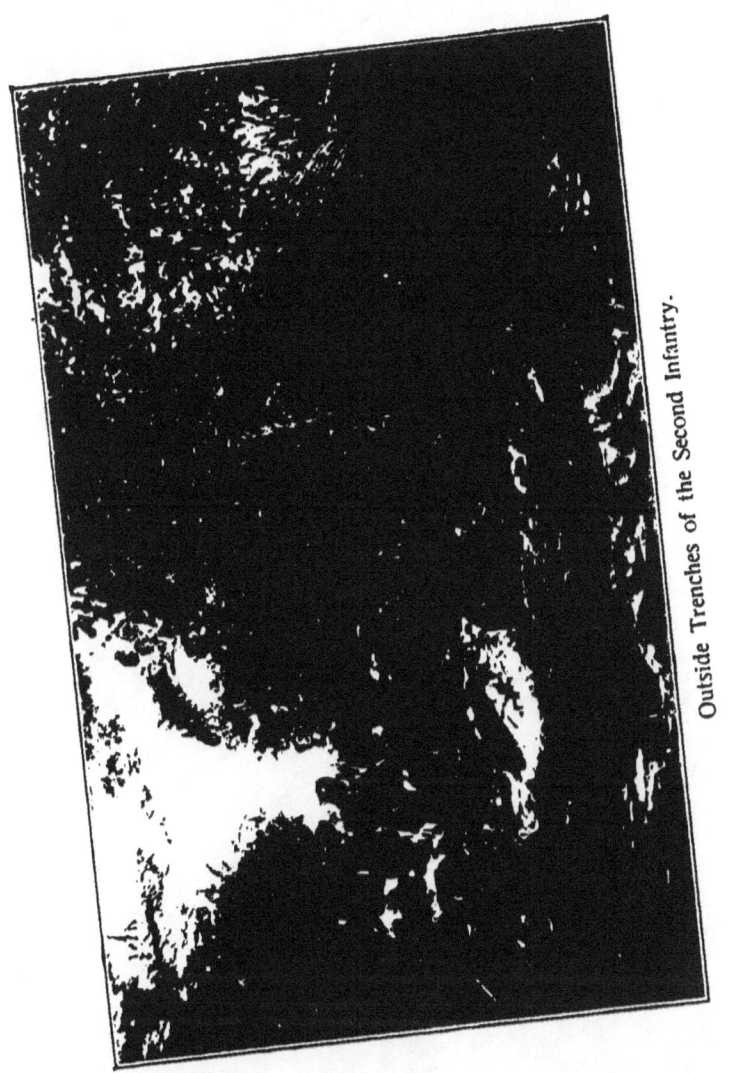

Outside Trenches of the Second Infantry.

were seldom more than a company at any one spot, and there were bare spaces from 100 to 200 yards apart held by only a dozen men. That night our soldiers did not sleep, as all of them were under fire, and many were kept at work enlarging the rifle-pits and digging fresh defences or standing guard. This work was inspired by General Wheeler, who sent to the rear for entrenching tools, and encouraged the brigade generals to make every effort to strengthen the position already won. In the morning Lawton's division, after a cruel night march from beyond El Caney, arrived at the rifle-pits and capped those hills farthest to the right. The firing continued viciously all that day; but our losses were small, while, as we learned later, the enemy's losses were exceedingly heavy. One of the Spanish prisoners said they amounted to over 1,000 in killed and wounded. When our men advanced up the trail on the morning of the battle they had been ordered to put their blanket rolls and haversacks in different places along the line of march, and details were left behind to guard these belongings. But a few hours later, when the wounded came straggling to the rear, the surgeons ordered these men who were on guard to help carry the wounded to the field hospitals, and so the two miles of ponchos and blankets and rations were abandoned along the trail, and everyone who passed up and down it helped himself to whatever he happened to need, and the Cubans to as much as they could carry. The result was that on the 2d of July the greater number of the men were still without shelter of any sort, and with almost nothing to eat.

That evening the now celebrated conference of the Generals was held at El Poso. The moonlight and the random firing which punctuated the silence of the night gave the meeting a dramatic and picturesque interest. Shafter lay on a door which had been taken from the El Poso farmhouse, and the other Generals stood around him whispering together. At some distance from them were their aides, and still farther removed were the men of General Shafter's cavalry escort, leaning with their elbows on their saddles, and wondering, as we all did, as to what the conference might bring forth. Those who took a part in it now say that the question of retreating from the position on the hills was discussed that night, but not seriously considered; but if it was not considered then, it was the one topic of the following morning.

IN THE RIFLE-PITS

The situation in the rifle-pits on the morning of the 3d was really most critical. One smelt disaster in the air. The alarmists were out in strong force and were in the majority. The enlisted men

Trench to Right of San Juan Block-house Occupied by American Troops. These troops are under a constant fire but reserving their ammunition.

had been without a night's sleep since 4 o'clock of June 30th. For the greater part of that time they had been under a constant fire. They had not been fed. They had no tobacco, which is much more necessary to the nerve than is food to the stomach. To avoid the enemy's fire they were forced to move about on their hands and knees. Their clothing was as wet as constant perspiration and dew and rain and the fording of the streams could make it. Through sitting bent double in the trenches their limbs and backs were stiff and cramped, and they were weakened by a fierce tropical sun. They were hanging to the crest of the San Juan hills by their teeth and finger-nails, and it seemed as though at any moment their hold would relax and they would fall. The Generals of division and of brigade were unanimous in declaring that the situation was most desperate, and that the Commanding-General must show himself at the front or ask to be relieved of his command. One of them said:

"It does not matter so much which one of us is in command, so long as someone is. But we can't go on this way, with no one in authority."

After a tour of the rifle-pits, where I learned what the different commanding officers thought of the situation, I wrote a long despatch to the *Herald* in which was set forth the serious nature of our position. This despatch was criticised later, on the ground that it had given information of our condition to the enemy. The same criticism could be made with equal justice of the despatch of the Commanding-General, who cabled on the 2d that his lines were so thin that he feared he might be forced to fall back—if that is not giving information to the enemy and of a most agreeable character, it has no meaning whatsoever. It was stated that my despatch which appeared on July 7th in the New York *Herald* had been recabled to the Paris *Herald*, that from Paris it was forwarded to Madrid, and that on the next day, July 8th, the authorities in Madrid communicated its contents to General Toral—so giving the garrison in Santiago increased confidence and hope, and encouraging it to hold out longer against us. It was even suggested that the writer should be shot for treason. It is most unpleasant to be accused of treason, and perhaps I may be allowed to point out now that on July 8th the garrison at Santiago offered to surrender. Hence, if the despatch ever reached Santiago, so far from giving the garrison hope and confidence and inspiring it with a desire to hold out longer, it either had no result whatsoever, or a result exactly opposite from the one it was suggested it would produce.

After Cervera's fleet was destroyed on the 3d the strain was perceptibly relaxed, the firing ceased, and we entered into a more cheerful state of existence under the white flag of truce. The rifle-pits from this time on were divided against themselves into two parties, one of which, without meaning to reflect upon it in any way, might be called the faction of the Alarmists. These gentlemen were peace-at-any-price men, and at one time their anxiety to finish off the campaign was so great that they seriously threatened the honor of the army and of the country by wishing to accept the original terms of General Toral's offer of evacuation. President McKinley's message, ordering them to accept nothing less than unconditional surrender, came to them like a sharp slap in the face, and filled the hearts of the younger officers and men with the greatest possible amusement and relief. The greater number of the alarmists were camped in a hollow between two hills, and the malarial nature of the low ground they occupied and the fact that they were constantly sleeping in a swamp seemed to prey upon their spirits and to give them a gloomy point of view. One of them, who was a constant prophet of evil, came up to General Lawton just as he arrived at the trenches after the long night march from El Caney, and in the hearing of the men pointed in great excitement to a distant hill and cried: "Do you see that hill, General Lawton? There is a battery of

The Trenches of the Fourth Infantry.

Spanish artillery hidden on that hill, and it enfilades all of your trenches. If it should open fire now, you would not have a man left alive."

Lawton's men had fought all the day before and marched all the previous night, and such statements from a colonel did not tend to improve their nerves. They looked at Lawton with anxious eyes, and he with charming readiness pretended to entirely misunderstand.

"Well, I cannot help it," he said, pulling off his gauntlets. "My men are too tired to capture that battery now, and I won't order them to do it; in an hour perhaps, when they are rested, I'll go over and take it, but there is no hurry."

The men turned away perfectly satisfied, and the alarmist is still wondering how General Lawton came to misunderstand.

The days that followed July 3d were filled with innumerable visits to the Spanish lines under flags of truce. To the men in the pits, who knew nothing of the exigencies of diplomacy, these virgin flags were as offensive as those of red are to the bull. The men had placed their own flags along the entire line of trenches; and though they afforded the enemy a perfect target and fixed our position as clearly as buoys mark out a race-course, the men wanted the flags there, and felt better at seeing them there, and so there they remained. The trenches formed a horseshoe curve five miles in length, and the entire line was defiantly decorated with our flags. When they fluttered in the wind at full length and the sun kissed their colors, they made one of the most inspiring and beautiful pictures of the war. The men would crouch for hours in the pits with these flags rustling above them, and felt well repaid for their service; but when they saw crawling across the valley below the long white flag of truce, their watchfulness seemed wasted, their vigilance became a farce, and they mocked and scoffed at the white flag bitterly. These flags were sent in so frequently that the men compared them to the different war extras of a daily paper, and would ask, "Has that ten o'clock edition gone in yet?" and, "Is this the base-ball edition coming out now, or is it an extry?"

One of the regulars said to me in great perplexity, "I can't make out this flag of truce gag. It reminds me of two kids in a street fight, stopping after every punch to ask the other fellow if he's had enough. Why don't we keep at it until somebody gets hurted?"

One of the cowboys of the Rough Riders expressed the same idea in professional phraseology:

"Now that we got those Mexicans corraled," he said, " why don't we brand them ? "

It really did seem as though we were a little too anxious, and our frequent attempts to feel the

Looking to the Left Down the Trench of the Second Infantry.

pulse of General Toral's courage by notes of hand instead of by gunpowder gave him more confidence than was good for him or for us. The navy would drop a few shells into Santiago, and at once an officer would be rushed into Toral's lines with a note inquiring whether he was not terribly frightened, and assuring him that that was nothing to what the navy could do if it tried, and did he not think he had better act nicely about it and surrender? To which Toral would reply airily that, on the contrary, he was far from frightened; that he knew our troops were suffering from fever while his own were acclimated, and that he was prepared to hold out against us indefinitely. So the next day we would fire a few cannon shots at him and rush in another flag of truce to inquire how he liked that, warning him that if he did not at once behave like a good boy we would eat him up at 10 o'clock the next morning. That was our ultimatum. But at 10 o'clock the next morning we would send in another flag to say that we would "extend his time" a few days longer, and that then we really would eat him up.

We extended Toral's time so frequently that it reminded Major-General Breckinridge of a story. General Breckinridge, as Inspector-General, held no active command. He represented the Commander-in-Chief at Washington, and his duty was just to sit around on a box of rations and make himself pleasant, and to observe things and report upon them later. He was a most charmingly inconsequent person, and the only one in the

Looking Toward Santiago from the Trenches in Front of the San Juan Block-house.

IN THE RIFLE-PITS

army who was never ruffled or bored or indignant, but, instead, was always politely amused and content. He told many stories, and told them exceedingly well. The stories were good in themselves, and it was invariably the case that you discovered later that they had summed up the situation in a line.

"A drunken man," so General Breckinridge related, "once considered himself insulted by John L. Sullivan, and, without recognizing who Sullivan was, gave him three minutes in which to apologize. Sullivan appreciated his opponent's condition and said, 'I don't need three minutes, I apologize now. What more will you have to drink?' and departed. When he had gone the barkeeper said to the man, 'Do you know who that was you wanted to fight just now?'

"The drunken man said he did not know, nor did he care.

"'Well, that was John L. Sullivan,' said the barkeeper, 'the champion pugilist of the world. Now what would you have done if he hadn't apologized in three minutes?'

"The drunken man gave the question a few moments' brief consideration. 'I guess I would have extended his time,' he said."

I lived in the rifle-pits from July 3d to 15th,

after both sides had appointed Peace Commissioners and the surrender was a fact. At headquarters they were just as uncomfortable as we were in the trenches and in much greater danger, as it was much easier to keep out of range on the hills than when approaching or leaving them along the trail. But the life in the rifle-pits was much more interesting than was that at head-quarters. We were in constant sight of the enemy, who was not more than three hundred yards distant; we could keep in better touch with our own men, and the different parleys and peace negotiations took place under our eyes.

The most interesting event which passed in view of the rifle-pits was the return of Lieutenant Hobson. Hobson had been a prisoner for six weeks. On some days we were told he was dead, but at last we were assured he was alive. From our pits we could see the walls of his jail; and he could see our five miles of fluttering flags crowding closer and closer to him every evening, and signalling him silent messages of hope and encouragement. Between his iron bars he could watch our men, moving along the yellow trenches or peering toward him through a field-glass, and the pickets—those tall gaunt regulars who had taken the hills with their blood and

The Spanish Prisoners being Escorted to the Lines to be Exchanged for Hobson and his *Merrimac* Crew.

who were now creeping up on him by night nearer and nearer, winning the ground between him and themselves by the sweat of their brows.

And one day, with the rifle-pits behind him filled with thousands of the enemy, with the rifle-pits before him filled with thousands of his friends, Hobson and his seven comrades rode out into the welcoming arms of the American army and into their inheritance.

The trail up which they came was a broad one between high banks, with great trees meeting in an arch overhead. For hours before they came officers and men who were not on duty in the rifle-pits had been waiting on these banks, broiling in the sun and crowded together as closely as men on the bleaching-boards of a base-ball field.

Hobson's coming was one of the most dramatic pictures of the war. The sun was setting behind the trail, and as he came up over the crest he was outlined against it under this triumphal arch of palms. The soldiers saw a young man in the uniform of the navy, his face white with the prison pallor, and strangely in contrast with the fierce tan of their own, and with serious eyes, who looked down at them steadily.

For a moment he sat motionless, and then the waiting band struck up "The Star-Spangled

Banner." No one cheered or shouted or gave an order, but every one rose to his feet slowly, took off hat slowly, and stood so, looking up at Hobson in absolute silence.

It was one of the most impressive things one could imagine. No noise, nor blare, nor shouted tribute could have touched the meaning or the depths of feeling there was in that silence.

And then a red-headed, red-faced trooper leaped down into the trail and shouted, "Three cheers for Hobson;" and the mob rushed at him with a roar of ecstasy, with a wild welcome of friendly cheers. Few men, certainly very few young men, have ever tasted such a triumph. These men who had made it possible for him to leave his cell and to breathe fresh air again were not of his branch of the service, they were not even brother officers, their attitude toward him was one of attention and salute, they were the men who had been gathered from every point of the Union to be drilled and hammered and fashioned into the thing called a regular. They were without local or political friends or conditions, they had no staff of artists and reporters at their heels to make them heroes in spite of themselves; but they were the backbone of the war—the professional fighting-machines, the grumbling, self-

Another View of the Spanish Prisoners on the way to be Exchanged.

Copyright, 1898 by J. C. Hemment.

respecting, working regulars. As brave men they honored a brave man; and this sun-tanned, dirty, half-starved, fever-racked mob of regulars danced about the educated, clever engineer as though the moment was his, and forgot that at the risk of their lives they had set him free, that the ground he rode over had been splashed with their blood.

There is always something humorous about a sailor ashore, and after the serious, earnest face of Hobson it was a comic relief to see six obstinate mules dragging an ambulance loaded with seven clean, smart blue-jackets, grinning and shouting and rolling over each other in glee. Everyone who had started to run after Hobson stopped to cheer them; but they refused to be lionized, and turned aside the cheers of the enlisted men by shouting: "Say, but you fellers didn't do a thing to them the other night!"

"Say, we heard you," they yelled, drowning out the cheers of the troopers. "Your shells fell right into our hospital yard. Say, but we wished we was with you, we did."

"They come in dead in carts."

"You couldn't see the street for them."

It was no time for choosing similes. Men were dancing up and down on the trenches and the hills, waving hats and shrieking. Officers were shouting Hobson's name. Photographers were leaping about, perpetuating a moment.

It was the same story all the way to Siboney. Every little group of soldiers we came across stood at attention at the unusual sight of a navy uniform. When they recognized the man they waved their hats and cheered.

Hobson was the first officer I had seen saluted in six days. Everyone had been too busy to salute. When he came to where the Seventy-first New York was mending a road, the men gave a yell and rushed waist-high through the river and stopped the cavalcade while they mobbed him, shaking both his hands and crowding so close that his horse could not move.

It was the most wonderful ride a young man of twenty-eight has ever undertaken—to ride through the enemy's country guarded by your own countrymen; on every side to hear cheers and approval; at every step to learn that your work was done, and well done; to know the weary days in jail were over; to feel the fresh air and see the great mountain-peaks and royal palms bending benediction under a soft blue sky.

But best of all, perhaps, was when he rode through the twilight and reached the coast and

Blindfolded Spanish Prisoners on the way to the Meeting-place between the Lines.

saw again in the offing the lights of the flag-ship, his floating home, and heard from across the water the jubilant cheers of the blue-jackets, who could not even see him, who did not know he had already arrived, but who cheered because they had heard he was coming, because he was free.

The kind and the degree of discomfort which our men endured in the rifle-pits was variously understood by those at home. These latter appreciated the conditions which existed on the San Juan hills according to whether they themselves had ever roughed it on hunting trips or in camp. Some said, airily, that such hardships were the lot of every soldier; others, with less experience and with hearts more tender, regarded the life on the hills as a month of torture. One mother in Richmond refused to leave that city during the heat of the summer because she could not bear to think that she was cool and comfortable while her son was sweating in the tropics; and you heard of others who fasted from the good things of the table because some relative before Santiago was without them. In Philadelphia a group of wealthy young women, each with a husband or brother at the front, stoically gave each other luncheons composed of bacon and hardtack, forgetting that the sauce of appetite and life in the open air makes bacon and hardtack as palatable as White Mountain cake. As was developed later, when the fever raged in every regiment, the life on the hills was not a healthy one; but the constant excitement and the unusual nature of

Artillery Entrenched.

our surroundings at the time made up for many things. The men themselves grumbled at this but little; and when they did grumble, it was not that their condition was so hard, but at the fact that so many of the evils of that condition were quite unnecessary. Of the necessaries of life, or what seemed necessaries when at home,

Hobson's *Merrimac* Crew Arriving within the American Lines, just After the Exchange.

Copyright, 1898, by J. C. Hemment.

IN THE RIFLE-PITS

both officers and men were quite destitute. They were like so many Robinson Crusoes on a desert island. The Spanish rifle-pits in front and the devastated country in the rear afforded them as few comforts as a stretch of ocean. For three years the land back of us toward Siboney had been successively swept by Cuban insurgents and Spanish columns. There was, in consequence, not a cow to give milk, nor even a stray hen to give eggs. The village of Sevilla, which one of the Boston papers described as having been taken by our troops with no loss of life, consisted of the two ruined walls of one house. The rest of the village was on the ground, buried under trailing branches and vines. There was not even a forgotten patch of potatoes or of corn. Mangoes (which the men fried, or ate raw, and by so doing made themselves very ill), limes, and running water was all that the country itself contributed to our support. Money had no significance whatsoever. For a Cuban pony, which in time of peace one can buy for fifteen dollars in gold, I offered one hundred and fifty dollars a week rent, promising to return the pony when the campaign was finished, and to throw in a McClellan saddle as well; and though this offer was made many times to many Cubans, I could not get the pony. Later, when everybody began to steal everything that the owner was not sitting upon at the time and guarding with a gun, it was possible to buy a horse for less money. In the trenches a match was so precious a possession that, when you saw a man light his pipe with one instead of at the cooks' fire, you felt as though you had seen him strike a child. Postage-stamps were, of course, unknown; and those who could not write "soldier's letter" on their envelopes had to give up corresponding. Writing-paper at one time became so scarce that orders and requisition papers were made out on the margins of newspapers and on scraps torn from note-books and on the insides of old envelopes.

The comic paragraphers found much to delight them in my cabled suggestions that the officers and men were suffering from want of a place to bathe and for clean clothes. Of course, bathing is an effeminate and unmanly practice, and the American paragrapher is right to discourage cleanliness wherever he finds it; but cleanliness is an evil, nevertheless, which obtains in our army, and those of the officers who were forced to wear the same clothes by night and by day for three weeks were so weak as to complain. One officer said, "I do not at all mind other men's clothes being offensive to me, but when I cannot go to sleep on account of my own it grows serious." This is not a pleasant detail, but it describes a condition which existed. The personal belongings of the officers had been left behind on the transports, and, as the pack-trains were sorely

San Juan Block-house—American Troops in Trenches.

needed to bring up the rations, they never saw razors and fresh linen again until they purchased them in Santiago. A tooth-brush was the only article of toilet to which all seemed to cling, and each of the men carried one stuck in his hat-band, until they appeared to be a part of the uniform. Nothing seemed so much to impress the foreign *attachés* as the passing of company after company of regulars, each with a tooth-brush twisted in his hat-band.

I lost my saddle-bags for three days, but they were found and returned to me by the surgeon of the Rough Riders. "There was nothing in the saddle-bags to identify you as the owner," he said, "but somebody told me you had lost yours, so I brought these over." His blue shirt happened to be unbuttoned as he spoke, and on the undershirt he wore I read "R. H. Davis." I pointed out this strange fact. "Davis," he cried, beseechingly, "there was fifty dollars of yours in those saddle bags and bacon and quinine, and we never touched them. We gave them all back, but that clean shirt I had to have. I'm only human. I will part with my life before I give you back that shirt." There was another story which illustrates the value of tobacco when it has ceased to exist. General Sumner owned a box of very bad Jamaica cigars. He was the only man in the Fifth Army Corps, except young Wheeler, who had any, so he was a marked man. In those days no one wore much insignia of rank; one of General Wheeler's stars was cut out of a tin cup, and Roosevelt's acorns were hammered from a leaden spoon. On the 30th of June,

IN THE RIFLE-PITS

Sumner was sitting by the trail without his blouse, in a blue shirt, and with no sign of rank about him, but he was smoking. He spoke rather sharply to a line of regulars who were hurrying forward.

"Who was that man spoke to you?" one of them asked the other over his shoulder.

"I dunno," said the regular. "But he's a general, for sure. He was smoking a cigar."

When it rained the water ran down the hills in broad streams, overflowing the tent-trenches and leaping merrily over the bodies of the men. It was not at all an unusual experience to sleep through the greater part of the night with the head lifted just clear of the water and the shoulder and one-half of the body down in it. Mr. Whigham, who lived at Shafter's head-quarters, and young Dr. Greenleaf, who visited them, told me of seeing the fever patients there lying in a hollow where the water ran over them in a continuous stream. During the week we were camped below El Poso, whenever it rained during the day both officers and men used to stow their clothes under the dog-tent in a rubber poncho and stand about naked until the sun came out again. I have a photograph of one of the officers of the Rough Riders digging his rain-trench while dressed in a gold chain and locket. General Miles was very much amused and startled when he visited the camp of the volunteers from Washington, D. C., to see several hundred of them standing naked at attention and saluting him as he passed. Quinine was very scarce, even before the fever set in, and boys, whose rich fathers in New York were spending many dollars in sending cables to inquire as to their safety and health, were going about begging for one quinine pill for a comrade.

During those days there was constant danger that a storm might set in and drive the transports out to sea and destroy the trails and cause the streams to overflow their banks, and so cut off the army from its base of supplies. There was a bridge across each of the two streams near the hills; but one was only an old gate which someone had found and thrown across the stream from bank to bank, and the other bridge was made of bamboo. The story was that when a Michigan regiment arrived at this stream on its way to the front, one of the volunteers who was a lumberman offered to throw a bridge across it in order to save the regiment from the wetting which would ensue if the men waded across it, as every one else had been doing for a week. This bridge of the lumberman was considered to be rather a joke on the Engineers, but they denied the truth of the story and claimed that they had built the bridge themselves. But as for seven days they had neglected to build any bridge over this stream, which was not more than ten feet wide, it does not much matter who did bridge it eventually. The absence of a bridge at this stream was very important, because fording it kept the men in a constant state of dampness, which helped bring on the fevers which followed later. The heavy storm on the morning of the 13th swept away the gate and the bamboo bridge, and the swollen stream overflowed its banks, delaying the pack-train with the rations and Captain Treat's artillery, and cutting off all direct communication with the transports. I am positive that there was no bridge until the 7th of July, for it was being built late on the afternoon of the 6th when we rode with Hobson to Siboney. The men working on it then told him it was not yet strong enough to bear the weight of his horse.

So much has been written about the Rough Riders that one approaches them with some hesitation, and in spite of the fact, and not on account of the fact, that they formed the most picturesque regiment in the army. They started in at the beginning of the war very heavily handicapped by too much advertising, and they had to live that down before the public would believe in them. But the notoriety the advertising gave

Trenches of the First Cavalry Before Santiago.

them made each man feel a sense of responsibility and *esprit de corps*, a feeling which existed to the same degree in no other regiment. This sentiment was encouraged by the officers, and among the men there was a most brotherly exhibition of loyalty and good-will and unselfishness. The hardest part of a campaign is, of course, not the fighting, but the inaction of the camp and the digging of drains and ditches, the standing guard over nothing in the sun or in the rain, and having to sleep in three inches of water or to make fires out of damp wood. It was the cheery spirit with which the Rough Riders performed these duties that distinguished them from the volunteers. While others grumbled and protested mutinously that they had volunteered to fight Spaniards and not to dig roads, the Rough Riders went about whatever duty was assigned to them promptly and in a cheerful spirit, and by binding a laurel to the plough made all manner of unpleasant duties a service of patriotism. They were just as much a source of interest to the regulars of the army before Santiago as they were later, on their return, to the civilians of Broadway, and to the generals the regiment was the *enfant terrible* of the trenches. The alarmists were in constant distress as to what they might do next, and actually feared that some bright morning this unique organization would slip its collar and charge the Spanish lines, alone and unsupported. As it was, they pushed their rifle-pits forward every night, and their redan held the men who were nearest to the enemy. On the 10th, when there was a brief bombardment, the dynamite gun which was attached to the Rough Riders' regiment upset a six-inch gun in the Spanish lines, and the Rough Riders leaped up on the trenches, and cheered, and gave their piercing cowboy yells. The noise was heard at Wheeler's head-quarters, and produced a momentary panic there, lest the noise meant that the cow-punchers and college boys had started on a run for Santiago. On the night that the First Illinois arrived at the front they were so anxious to get into action that as soon as darkness fell they began firing at everything that moved, and among other things at the pickets in front of the pits of the Rough Riders. The Captain in charge of the outpost sent back word to the Colonel of the First Illinois that, if his men shot at his detail again, he would be under the painful necessity of capturing the Colonel's trenches.

While writing of the Rough Riders I wish to speak of one of them whom I knew but slightly, but whom I saw constantly about the camp and on the march, and whom I admired more as a soldier than almost any other man in the regiment. This was Sergeant Tiffany, who, by tradition and previous environment, was apparently the least suited of men to perform the work he was ordered to do. But he played the part given him as well

IN THE RIFLE-PITS

as it could have been played. He was the ideal Sergeant, strict in discipline to himself and to others, doing more than his share of the day's work sooner than leave the work ill-done, never stooping to curry favor from his men, but winning

Lieutenant William Tiffany.

it by force of example, and smiling with the same cheerful indifference when an intrenching tool made his hands run with blood, or a Spanish bullet passed through his hat, as one did when he charged the hill at San Juan. He stood at salute and took his orders from men with whom for many years he had been a college-mate and a club-mate, recognizing in them only his superior officers; and there was not a mule-skinner or cow-puncher in the regiment that did not recognize in him something of himself and something finer and better than himself. When Roosevelt promoted him to a lieutenancy for bravery at the battle of San Juan, I heard him say:

"Tiffany, I am especially glad to give you this step, because you are about the only man who has never by sign or word acted as though he thought he deserved promotion. There are some who are always very busy whenever I pass, and who look at me as though they meant to say, 'See how humble I am, and how strictly I attend to my duties. You who know how important a person I am at home will surely recognize this and make me an officer.' But you have never acted as though you expected to be anything but a Sergeant all your life, and you have done your work as though you had been a Sergeant all your life, and so I am glad of this chance to make you a Lieutenant.

Death, which had so often stepped back to let Tiffany pass forward with his men, touched him when it came with that same courtesy which he had always shown to others, taking him when those

Raising the Flag Over Santiago.

Drawn by F. C. Yohn from photographs and sketches made during the ceremony by Mr. Archibald. Showing the squadron of Second United States Cavalry and Ninth United States Infantry and the group of general officers and their staffs.

nearest to him in heart were near him in person. But his life was given to his country as much as though he had lost it in the cactus of Guasimas, or on the hill of San Juan, or in the rifle-pits when he stood for hours behind his quick-firing gun. He was a gentle and brave man, an obedient sergeant and a masterful officer, a soldier who never "shirked a duty, nor sought an honor."

I did not see the ceremony of the raising of our flag over Santiago. The surrender itself had become an accomplished fact, and, as the campaign in Porto Rico promised better things, I left the rifle-pits when General Miles sailed for Juanica, and landed with our troops at that first port.

The life in the rifle-pits was a most interesting and curious experience, and one full of sad and fine and humorous moments, but on looking back at it now the moments which one remembers best, and which one will remember the longest are, I think, those which came at sunset when the band played the national anthem. The men would be bending over the fires cooking supper or lying at length under the bomb-proofs stretching limbs cramped with two hours' watch in the pits, the officers would be seated together on a row of wooden boxes, and beyond the mountains the setting sun lit the sky with a broad red curtain of flame; and then to these tired, harassed, and hungry men would come the notes of the "Star-Spangled Banner," which bore with it something of a call to arms and something of a call to prayer. Those who have heard it and who have cheered it in the hot crowded theatres, in the noisy city streets, cannot really know or understand it. They must hear it very far away from home, with great palm-trees giving it an unfamiliar background, with a listening enemy a few hundred yards distant, with the sense of how few of your own people are about you, and how cut off they are, and how dependent upon one another. As the instruments beat out the notes each night the little discomforts of the day cease to exist, the murmurs of the rifle-pits, which were like the hum of a great bazaar, were suddenly silent, and the men before the fires rose stiffly from their knees, and those in the gravelike trenches stood upright, and the officers stepped from their tents into the sight of the regiment. On every hill, as far as one could see, rows and rows of motionless figures stood facing the direction from which the music came, with heads uncovered and with eyes fixed on the flags that rose above the hills where their hands had placed them.

When the music had ceased, the men pulled on

The Trenches of the Rough Riders on San Juan Hill.

Sergeant Tiffany's Colt gun may be seen, to the left, under the Rough Riders' flag. The flag on the right belongs to the Tenth Colored Regulars. The Spanish block-house seen above the trench was only three hundred yards distant.

their hats again and once more began to fry a piece of hardtack in a layer of grease and fat; but for a moment they had seen the meaning of it all, they had been taken outside of themselves and carried back many miles to the country for which they fought, and they were inspired with fresh courage and with fresh resolve.

John Fox, Jr., War Correspondent.

CHAPTER VIII

THE PORTO RICAN CAMPAIGN

Seal of the Corporation of the City of Ponce after the Occupation of the United States. The original seal contained the arms of Ponce, a lion on a bridge.

WHEN the men who accompanied our army to Porto Rico returned to their own people again, they found that at home the Porto Rican campaign was regarded as something in the way of a successful military picnic, a sort of comic-opera war, a magnified field-day at Van Cortlandt Park. This point of view was hardly fair, either to the army in Porto Rico or to the people at home. It cheated the latter of their just right to feel proud.

In comparison to the Santiago nightmare, the Porto Rican expedition was a *fête des fleurs;* but the reason for this, apart from the fact that the country, unlike Cuba, had not been devastated and that the Porto Ricans, unlike the Cubans, were most friendly, was one which should make all Americans pleased with themselves and with

The *Gloucester* Bombarding Juanica, Porto Rico.

Copyright by E. C. Kost, New York.

their army. It should give them such confidence in the army and its generals as we like to honestly feel when we boast of anything to which we can prefix the possessive pronoun, whether it be our local base-ball nine, our express trains or elevators, or our army and navy.

Porto Rico was a picnic because the commanding generals would not permit the enemy to make it otherwise. The Spaniards were willing to make it another nightmare—they were just as ready to kill in Porto Rico as in Cuba—but our commanding General in Porto Rico was able to prevent their doing so. A performance of any sort always appears the most easy when we see it well done by an expert—even golf looks possible as Whigham plays it. All he does is to hit a ball with a stick. But you might go out and hit the same ball with the same stick for a year, and no one would think of giving you silver cups. Anyone who has seen a really great matador face a bull in a bull-ring has certainly thought that the man had gained his reputation easily. He walks about as unconcernedly as you walk about your room; and when he is quite ready he waits for the bull, takes a short step to one side, thrusts his sword into the bull's neck, and the bull is dead. The reason the Spanish bull gored our men in Cuba and failed to touch them in Porto Rico was entirely due to the fact that Miles was an expert matador; so it is hardly fair to the commanding General and the gentlemen under him to send the Porto Rican campaign down into history as a picnic.

This is not saying that it was not a picnic, but explaining why it was so. A general who can make an affair of letting blood so amusing to his men that they regard it as a picnic is an excellent general.

One of the lesser evils of the Cuban campaign was that it gave our friends, the enemy in Europe, the idea that the way in which that particular expedition was conducted was typical of the way every other expedition would be conducted which we might send over sea. But should they act seriously on that idea, they would find themselves abruptly and painfully undeceived. The European can say, to our discredit, that we failed to feed our soldiers in the field, and to care for them when they were wounded and ill; but they cannot say that the soldiers did not do their share, even though republics were ungrateful and political officials incompetent.

Even our own people had just cause to be alarmed at the bungling and waste of life in

General Miles in Launch of *Massachusetts* Towing Pontoons, at Juanica, Porto Rico.

Copyright by E. C. Rost, New York.

Cuba. So it might be well, both at home and abroad, to emphasize at once the fact that we have other generals in the field.

That the people do not know more concerning the Porto Rican expedition is partly due to the fact that the majority of newspaper correspondents were detained in Cuba by sickness and quarantine, and that those who reached the island were too few in number to give the expedition there the *acclaim* it deserved. For three days there were only two correspondents with the army in Porto Rico, and never more at any time than eighteen. In Cuba there were more than a hundred. Moreover, the campaign was nipped by peace almost before it could show its strength; but from the start it was one with which any of the great military powers would have been pleased and satisfied. And this in spite of the fact that the regiments engaged, with but three exceptions, were composed of volunteers.

The army in Porto Rico advanced with the precision of a set of chessmen; its moves were carefully considered and followed to success; its generals, acting independently and yet along routes reconnoitered by General Roy Stone and Major Flagler, and selected by General Miles, never missed a point nor needlessly lost a man,

THE CUBAN AND PORTO RICAN CAMPAIGNS

nor retreated from a foot of land over which they had advanced. And two months before the army had reached the island Captain Whitney, at the greatest personal risk a man can run, had carefully studied out the entire island, its roads and harbors, so that not only the army, but the navy also, relied upon and used his drawings and notes. Every day the four different columns swept the Spaniards before them in a net, capturing town after town and company after company. Their fights were but skirmishes, but the skirmishes were as carefully thought out, and the enemy was as scientifically surrounded, attacked, and captured, as though great battles had been fought and thousands of lives lost in accomplishing the same end. There was more careful preparation and forethought exhibited in the advances which our generals made upon the little towns that they captured in Porto Rico, than was shown in the entire campaign against the city of Santiago—General Chaffee's reconnoissance and

Captain Henry H. Whitney.

capture of El Caney alone always excepted. The courage of the men is not under discussion now; what we are considering here is a comparison of good generalship with bad, and the American reader, for his own satisfaction, should not belittle a clean-cut, scientific campaign by calling it a picnic. He should remember that in Porto Rico eight cities and towns, with 100,000 inhabitants, were won over to the United States at the cost of very few men killed. Santiago, with its 40,000 inhabitants, was won for the Cubans at the cost of thousands of men killed and wounded in battle and wrecked by fever. An eye-witness of both campaigns must feel convinced that the great success of the one in Porto Rico was not due to climatic advantages and the co-operation of the natives, but to good management and good generalship.

Juanica is a pretty little harbor protected by very high cliffs. The town is one street, which runs back for a mile under the shade of crimson trees, with houses of gay colors on either side of it. Back of the one street are lanes crowded with huts of palm-leaves. The *Gloucester* ran into the harbor and fired a three-pounder at a Spanish flag on a block-house. This was the first intimation that anyone, except General Miles,

THE CUBAN AND PORTO RICAN CAMPAIGNS

had received that the American troops were to land on the south coast of Porto Rico. When the news reached Washington the War Department was surprised, because it thought that General Miles would land at Fajardo, in the north; the Spaniards were surprised as a matter of course; and the newspaper boats were so overtaken with surprise that, with one exception, none of them hove in sight for three days.

The first landing was made by the blue-jackets of the *Gloucester*. They built a trocha of stones and barbed wire across the one street, and called it Fort Wainwright, and killed four Spaniards with a Colt's quick-firing gun. Then they wigwagged for reinforcements, and the regulars of the artillery and the engineers under Lieutenant-Colonel Black came in to give them countenance. Meanwhile, the *Gloucester* fired at the ridges about the harbor and a troop of cavalry on a hill, and, as she was short-handed, the Paymaster and the Surgeon helped to feed the guns. It can be truly said that life on the *Gloucester* was seldom dull. When the Spaniards had fled, 2,000 volunteers from Massachusetts and Illinois, and more regulars of the artillery, were put on shore, and in a few hours were camped along the street;

United States Artillery Entering Ponce.
Photographed by the author.

and the inhabitants, who had fled to the hills before the hideous bombardment of the *Gloucester's* three-pounder, returned again to their homes. The Porto Ricans showed their friendliness to the conquerors by selling horses to the officers at three times their value, and the volunteers made themselves at home on the doorsteps of the village, and dandled the naked yellow babies on their knees, and held marvellous conversations with the natives for hours at a time, in a language entirely their own, but which seemed to be entirely satisfactory. The next morning there was an outpost skirmish, in which the Sixth Massachusetts behaved well, and the next evening there was a false alarm from the same regiment. This called out the artillery and the Illinois regiment, and the picture made by the shining brown guns as they bumped through the only street in the moonlight was sinister and impressive. To those of us who had just come from Santiago the sight of the women sitting on porches and rocking in bent-wood chairs, the lighted swinging lamps with cut-glass pendants, and the pictures and mirrors on the walls which we saw that night through the open doors as we rode out to the pickets, seemed a part of some long-forgotten existence. We know now that the women were dark of hue and stout, that the pictures were chromos of the barber-shop school, and that the swinging lamps were tawdry and smoked horribly; but at that moment, so soon after the San Juan rifle-pits, the women of Juanica were as beautiful as the moonlight, and their household gods of the noblest and best.

The alarm turned out to be a false one, and, except for the pleasure the spectacle had afforded the fat, brown ladies on the porches, the men had lost half a night's sleep to no purpose. Later, they lost the other half of the night because our outposts on the hills would mistake stray mules and cattle for Spaniards, and kept up an unceasing fire about the camp until sunrise. Some of their bullets hit the transport on which General Miles was sleeping, and also the ship carrying the Red Cross nurses, who were delighted at being under fire, even though the fire came from the Sixth Illinois. From remarks made the next morning by General Miles, he did not seem to share in their delight.

After three days, General Guy Henry moved on to occupy Juaco, and General Miles proceeded down the coast to the Port of Ponce. The city of Ponce, which lies two miles back from the port, surrendered officially and unofficially on four separate occasions. It was possessed of the surrender habit in a most aggravated form. Indeed, for anyone in uniform it was most unsafe to enter the town at any time, unless he came prepared to accept its unconditional surrender. In the official account sent to Washington by Captain Higginson of the *Massachusetts*, the city of Ponce and the port surrendered to Commander Davis of the *Dixie*—so General Miles reported; so history, as it is written, will report. But, as a matter of fact, the town first surrendered to Ensign Curtin of the *Wasp*, then to three officers who strayed into it by mistake, then to Commander Davis, and finally to General Miles. Ensign Curtin is a grandson of the war governor of Pennsylvania. He is about the youngest-looking boy in the navy, and he is short of stature, but in his methods he is Napoleonic. He landed with a letter for the military commander, which demanded the surrender of the port and city, and he wore his sidearms and an expression in which there was no trace of pity. The Captain of the Port informed him that the military commander was at Ponce, but that he might be persuaded to surrender if the American naval officer would condescend to drive up to Ponce and make his demands in person. The American officer fairly shook and quivered with indignation. "Zounds," and "Gadzooks," and "Damme, sir," would have utterly failed to express his astonishment. Had it come to this, then, that an Ensign holding the President's commission, and representing such a ship of

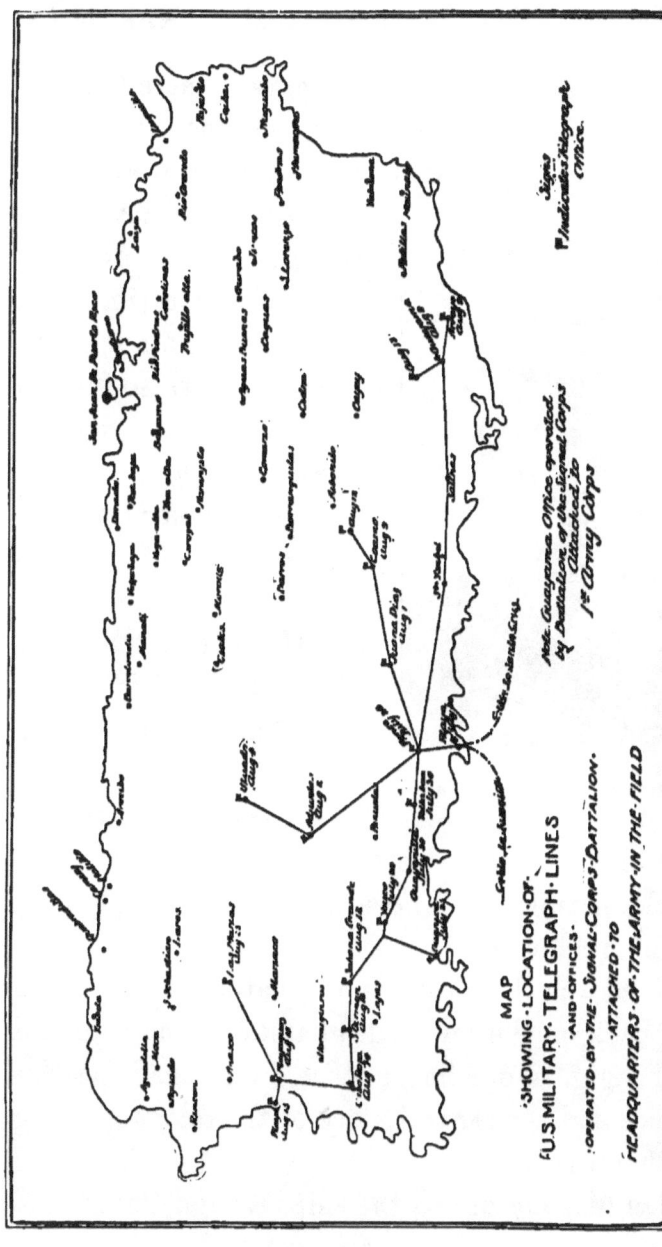

terror as the *Wasp,* was to go to a mere Colonel, commanding a district of 60,000 inhabitants?

"How long will it take that military commander to get down here if he hurries?" demanded Ensign Curtin. The trembling Captain of the Port, the terrified foreign consuls and the customhouse officials thought that a swift-moving cab might bring him to the port in a half-hour.

Ensign Curtin of the *Wasp.*

"Have you a telephone about the place?" asked the Napoleonic Curtin. They had.

"Then call him up and tell him that if he doesn't come down here in a hack in thirty minutes and surrender, I shall bombard Ponce!"

This was the Ensign's ultimatum. He turned his back on the terrified inhabitants and returned to his gig. Four hacks started on a mad race for Ponce and the central office of the telephone rang with hurry-calls.

On his way out to the ship, Ensign Curtin met

Troops Entering Ponce.

Drawn from a photograph taken by the author.

Commander Davis on his way to the shore. Commander Davis looked at his watch. "I shall ex-

General Miles and Staff in the Patio of the Hotel Français at Ponce

tend his time another half-hour," said Commander Davis. Ensign Curtin saluted sternly, making no criticism upon this weak generosity on the part of his superior officer, but he could afford to be magnanimous. He, at least, had upheld the honor of the navy, and he will go down in the history of the war as the middy who demanded and obtained a surrender by telephone.

General Miles landed in the morning after Curtin had taken the place, and Mr. Curtin came ashore in the same boat with us. We asked him if he had already landed, and he replied, modestly, that he had; but he spared the commanding General's feelings by making no reference to his own part in the surrender. In the boat with General Miles were the two head-quarters flags of the commanding General of the army, four officers of his personal staff, Curtin, and four regulars. One of these regulars spoke three languages, and as a soldier of the Foreign Legion of France had carried the first French flag to the shore of Tonquin. Although this was not known until later, one of the head-quarters flags of the United States army was handed to him to carry to the shore of Porto Rico. When one remembers that there are 25,000 regulars in our army to whom it might have been given, it was a curious coincidence that this particular honor should have fallen to that particular man. He was in no way unappreciative of the honor. He stood up in the bow and waved the heavy silk flag from one side to the other until the

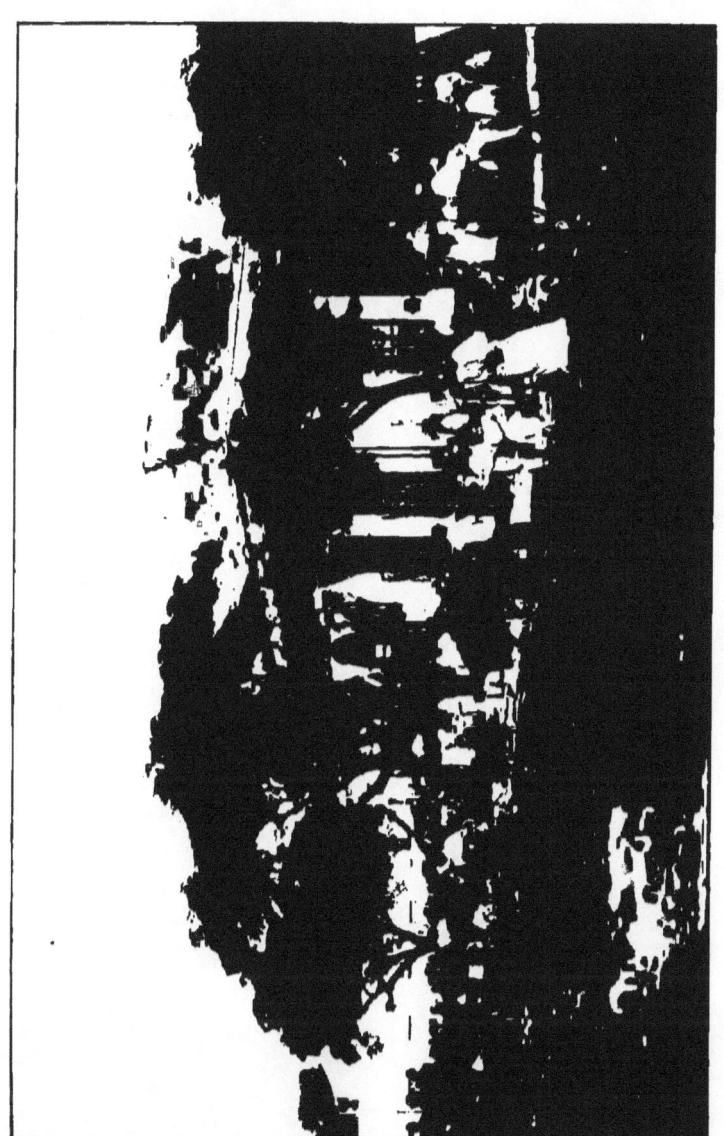

Market Place at Ponce.

boat rocked, and at the sight the several thousand people who were waiting for General Miles on the wharves and housetops and swamping the small boats in the wake of his gig shouted "Vivas" and shrieked and cheered. Suddenly the Franco-American soldier held up the flag as high as he could place it, and in most excellent and eloquent Spanish called upon the people of Porto Rico to welcome the commanding General of the United States. There was a momentary hush of surprise that an American soldier should show such knowledge of their own tongue, and then a wilder burst of "Vivas," and another pause to hear if there was more to follow. There was much more to follow. From the bow of our boat our self-elected orator assured them that the coming of General Miles brought them liberty, fraternity, peace, happiness, and wealth. He promised them no taxes, freedom of speech, thought, and conscience, "three acres and a cow," plurality of wives, "one man, one vote," and to every citizen a political office and a pension for life. Before the gig had touched the landing-steps the United States Government, in the person of that soldier, was pledged to give Porto Rico everything in its power and beyond its power to grant. So General Miles landed in triumph.

After that speech it is small wonder that Americans were popular in Porto Rico.

Later in the day, General Miles and General Wilson, in full dress uniform, received the homage of Ponce from the balcony of the Alcalde's pal-

Crossing the River Rio Bucana.

ace. Nothing could have been more enthusiastic or more successful than their open-air reception. The fire companies paraded in their honor, and ran over three of their own men, which gave the local Red Cross people an opportunity to appear on the scene, each man wearing four red crosses, to carry away the wounded. This created

THE PORTO RICAN CAMPAIGN

some confusion, as the firemen preferred to walk, but the Red Cross people were adamant, and bore them off on stretchers whether they would or no. The only thing wanting to complete the picture was an American flag. It was only a detail, but

American Soldier Showing a Rifle to Spaniards.

the populace seemed to miss it. It was about the only article with which the expedition was not supplied. Frantic cabling to Washington repaired the loss, and within a week flags were sent out all over the island and raised upon the roof of many a city hall. Ponce itself held more foreign flags than we had ever seen. Judging from their number, one would have thought that the population was composed entirely of English, Germans, French, and Swiss, and members of the Red Cross Society. It was explained later that the Spanish residents had been assured that the American soldiers would loot their houses, and so for their better protection they had invited all of their friends who were subjects of foreign powers to come and spend a few days and bring their flags with them. On one very handsome house belonging to a very rabid Spaniard, who apparently had a surfeit of spare bedrooms, there were as many flags as there are powers in the European concert. He was taking no chances.

The first week of the American occupation of Ponce, when new conditions arose every hour, was full of interest. There were financial questions to be answered, as to the rate of exchange and the collection of taxes and customs dues—questions of local law as opposed to martial law. There were Spanish volunteers swearing allegiance to the United States, and Porto Ricans to be sworn in as judges and registrars. The American post-office opened for business, telephone wires which had been cut for strategic reasons were repaired for the public service, the railroad was set in motion at the point of the

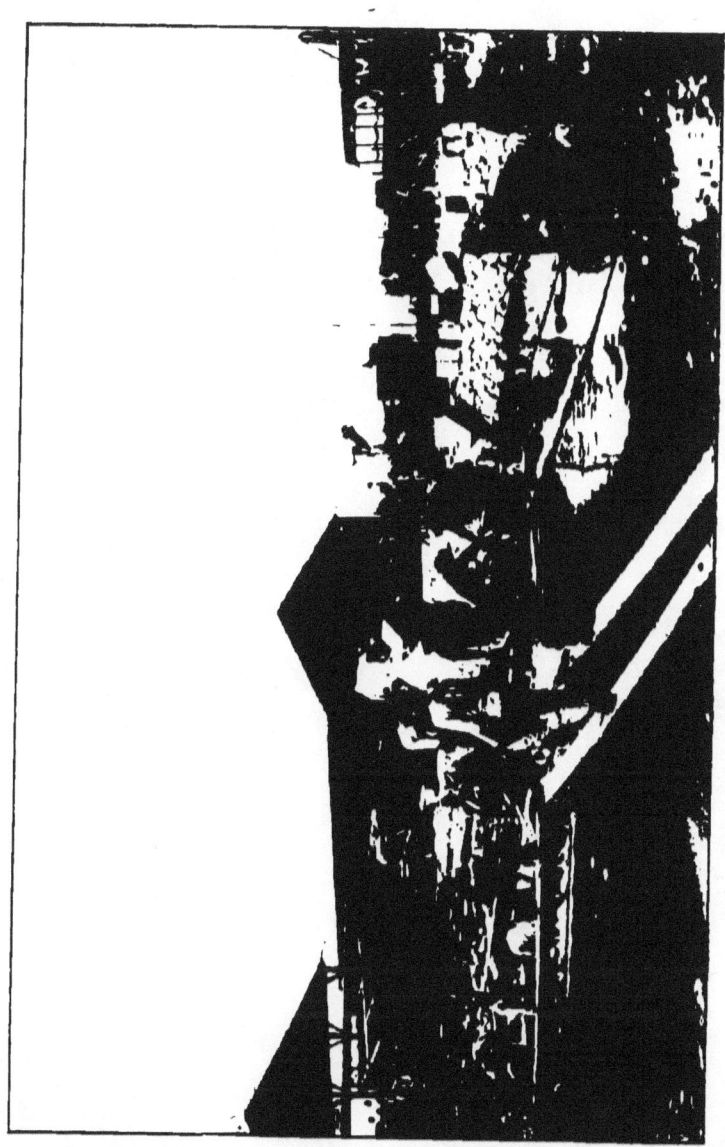
Unloading Army Supplies from the Transports at Port Ponce.

bayonet, and signs reading "English spoken here" were hung outside of every second shop. In the band-stand in the Plaza, where for many years the Spanish military band had played every Sunday and Thursday, the provost-guards slept and cooked and banged on a hoarse rheumatic piano. "Rosy O'Grady" and "The Banks of the Wabash" superseded "The March of Isabella" of the three nights previous, and an American company reopened the opera-house with a variety performance; a newspaper called *La Nueva Era* was issued in twenty-four hours, printed half in Spanish and half in English; and twenty miles out, at Coamo, where two roads met, an energetic volunteer who combined enterprise with patriotism nailed up a sign with a hand pointing North and reading:

```
GO TO JAMES GETTS
FOR CLOTHING,
WARRINGTON, WIS.
```

The people of Ponce were certainly the most friendly souls in the world. Nothing could surpass their enthusiasm or shake their loyalty. If a drunken soldier, of whom there were surprisingly few, entered the shop or home of a Porto Rican, the owner could not be persuaded to make a charge against him. The natives gave our men freely of everything; and the richer and better class of Porto Ricans opened a Red Cross hospital at their own expense and contributed money, medicines, cots, and doctors for our sick soldiers. They also placed two American Red Cross nurses in charge, and allowed them absolute authority.

Peace came too soon to allow the different generals who were making the ways straight to show all that they could do and how well they could do it. In view of this fact it was almost a pity that peace did come so soon. For with the bungling at Santiago, and the scandal and shame after the war of the treatment of our sick soldiers on the transports and in the fever camps, the successes which would have followed the advance of the different expeditions across Porto Rico would have been a grateful relief. The generals, with the exception of General Schwan, were handicapped to a degree by the fact that their commands were, for the greater part, composed of volunteers; but the personality of the generals, each in his different way, made this count for little, and they obtained as good ser-

City Troop Marching through the Town of Santa Isabel.

vice out of the men as the work that there was to do demanded. Particularly good was the service of Troop C of Brooklyn who for four days held the farthest out-post at Aibonito where they were under fire from quick-firing guns on the hills above them, and of the First City Troop of Philadelphia which well upheld the traditions of an organization which dates from the days of General Washington. It was not in the field alone, where they were on their native heath, that the generals distinguished themselves; but in governing and establishing order in the towns which they captured, where their duties were both peculiar and foreign to their experience, they showed to the greatest advantage. They went about the task of setting up the new empire of the United States as though our army had always been employed in seizing islands and raising the flag over captured cities. They played the conquerors with tact, with power, and like gentlemen. They recognized the rights of others and they forced others to recognize their rights. Wherever it was possible to do so, General Miles propitiated the people by employing local labor. Within an hour after the firing had ceased in Juanica, he was renting ox-carts and oxen from the native ranch-owners and buy-

Arrest of a Spanish Spy in Ponce. The man is holding his hands across his forehead in sign of surrender.

Drawn from a photograph taken by the author.

ing cattle outright. At Ponce he employed hundreds of local stevedores who had been out of work for many days. He set them to unloading the transports and coaling the war-ships; and when he learned that the boss stevedores were holding back part of the men's pay he corrected the abuse at once, and saw that each man received what was due to him. General Wilson, in his turn, as military governor of the city and district of Ponce, was confronted with many strange conditions. He had to invent oaths of allegiance, to tranquillize the foreign consuls, to protect rich Spaniards from too enthusiastic Porto Ricans, to adopt a new seal for the city, and a new rate of exchange; to appoint new officers in the courts, to set free political prisoners, and to arrest and lock up political offenders against the new régime.

But the work was not confined to the cities, and soon each of the generals had changed the magistrate's chair for the saddle. It was a beautiful military proposition, as General Miles laid it down. Four columns were to traverse the island from four different directions, and drive all the enemy outside of San Juan back into that city, so leaving none but friends on the flanks and in the rear. By taking all the towns *en route* and picking up every Spaniard it met on the way, the army would surround San Juan with the island already won. Then with the navy in the harbor and the army camped about the city,

THE CUBAN AND PORTO RICAN CAMPAIGNS

San Juan would, as a matter of common sense, surrender.

Peace interfered with the completion of this

City Troop on Road between Guayana and Ponce. Resting the horses.

plan, but its inception and start were most brilliant and successful. General Wilson was sent down the centre along the military road with directions to follow it straight on to the capital.

THE PORTO RICAN CAMPAIGN

On the right end of the rush-line, General Brooke and General Hains were to swing around to take Guayana and strike the military road back of Cayey and Aibonito just as Wilson closed up on

General Wilson Entering Coamo.
Photographed by the author.

these towns from the south. General Roy Stone, with a mixed command of Porto Ricans, United States volunteers and regulars, was sent to Adjuntas to reconnoitre and clear the way. General Guy Henry was sent out to follow the same route and to take the city of Arecibo in the north. On the extreme left, General Schwan, with a splendid command composed entirely of regulars, was given a sort of roving commission to fight anything he saw, and then to take Mayaguez and beat up toward Arecibo to join Henry. As soon as those columns were on the way, General Miles was to follow wherever his advice and presence would be of the most value.

The generals lost no time in getting to work. Juana Dias was, in theatrical parlance, a one-night stand, and it surrendered without a fight to General Wilson, but the taking of Coamo, the next city on his list, was one of the prettiest skirmishes of the campaign.

General Hains meanwhile had taken Guayana from four hundred Spaniards at the cost of one officer and four men wounded, all of the Fourth Ohio. On the 13th, General Schwan's regulars found the Spaniards intrenched in force at Las Marias and drove them back and out of Mayaguez, a city of 30,000 inhabitants. In this fight, two privates were killed and fourteen enlisted men and Lieutenant Byron were wounded. The Spanish loss was thirty in killed and wounded, and the Lieutenant-Colonel, with fifty privates,

City Troop Marching on Road between Ponce and Guayana.

were taken prisoners. General Stone engaged the enemy in a night skirmish beyond Adjuntas and drove the Spaniards back, carrying their killed

Third Wisconsin Entering Coamo.
Drawn from a photograph taken by the author.

and wounded with them. There was no loss among his own men.

The city of Coamo was taken by the Sixteenth Pennsylvania Volunteers, but it surrendered first to four correspondents who had galloped into it by mistake.

There was no reveille on the morning of the day the Sixteenth Pennsylvania took Coamo. At General Wilson's head-quarters a sentry shook the flaps of the tents and told us it was time to get up. He reminded one of a Pullman-car porter shaking the curtains of a berth and saying, "Only twenty minutes to New York." It was so unmilitary that everyone refused to wake.

So General Wilson taught the officers of his staff a lesson in punctuality by riding off without them, and they had to gallop three miles to overtake him.

The road was better than any road outside of the city parks in America, with a hard, sloping surface and rain-gutters at each side and brick bridges over the streams. It was shaded by pink and red trees and a few common or garden-trees of green, so that we might not think we were passing beneath a succession of triumphal arches. Sometimes on our right, above the sugar-cane, we saw the sea and the white spray breaking on the reefs.

As the cavalcade passed, the Porto Ricans came out lazily to the roadside and peered at the officers over the fences of cactus, and neglected,

The Women of Coamo Receiving the American Soldiers.
Photographed by the author.

brown, naked children fell out of the doors and bumped down the steps, howling dismally. The white helmet of the general was still half a mile ahead, and the sabre-tache of his aide was beating his horse's flanks like a club. The hoofs of our horses rang like hammers on the road, and the swords and picket-pins clattered and jangled. There were great hills to the left, and right, clothed with a hundred shades of green, and below them green lakes of sugar-cane, with the corrugated iron roofs and the tall chimneys of the sugar-mills rising out of them, and looking like turtle-back steamers pushing their way through the fresh water lakes.

As we raced by we saw teams of six oxen pulling long ploughs through chocolate-colored earth. Small boys rode one of each yoke of oxen and sang in chorus a drowsy, droning song, which sounded like the song the Lascars sing on a P. and O. steamer when they pull on a rope. The morning was very still, for there are few birds in Porto Rico, and only the hum of innumerable insect-life answered the ring of the horses' hoofs.

The white helmet of the general halted next to an open field of high, yellow grass, where four brown guns pointed at a block-house on the hill above Coamo. As we drew up one of the guns roared and flashed, and a cloud of white smoke rushed forward and stopped as though it had struck a solid wall and then swept back again, hiding the gun and the men about it in a curtain of mist. The horses under the trees reared and tugged at their bridles and danced, and terrified human beings came running up the road carrying their children and shying like the horses whenever a shot was fired. A few Mauser rifles answered the guns, but the bullets flew high and did no harm.

The block-house smoked and crumbled and then burst into red flames. The artillery limbered up again and crawled off up a hill to the right, and Troop C, of Brooklyn, moved off still farther to the right and disappeared over a hill. All the infantry started forward. It advanced in beautiful order, with scouts and skirmishers beating through the high grass and creeping up behind rocks and popping up suddenly from over the crests of the hills. In the level plain at the left of the road the regiments moved in blocks of blue and brown.

The men in blue made a target just twice as conspicuous as that made by the men in brown. But there was no one at hand to fire on them. On the other side of Coamo the Spaniards were hurrying across the bridge and out into the white road. On the hills above them the Sixteenth Regiment of Pennsylvania were waiting for them and opened fire. The enemy had not thought of an ambush. He had delayed until the first shot

Colonel Biddle, of General Wilson's Staff, Interrogating a Spanish Prisoner. Other prisoners under guard in the background.
Drawn from a photograph taken by the author.

from the artillery had broken the stillness of the morning, and then, feeling sure of an hour's start, had fallen back rapidly toward Aibonito. The Spaniards ran off the road into the rain gutters, and these, with the cactus lining the road, served as trenches. Their white hats were the mark at which the volunteers fired.

The Spanish comandante seemed to wish to die. He galloped out of the road and into the meadow, where he was conspicuous from the top of his head to the hoofs of his horse. At one time he stood motionless, where there was a break in the cactus hedge, holding his reins easily and looking up at the firing line above. After he was killed the men in the trench along the road raised a white handkerchief on a stick and ceased firing.

Colonel Biddle, of the engineers, who had acted as a scout for the volunteers, stood out on the edge of the hill and held a rifle above his head with both hands and let it fall. The Spaniards stepped into the road and repeated his motions, raising the rifles and dropping them to their feet. There were ten dead, ten wounded and one hundred and sixty taken prisoners. Ten of the Sixteenth were wounded.

The volleys had been heard on the other side of the town, and the artillery fired three more shots for moral effect only. The infantry, hurrying to the rescue, found that the bridge on the Ponce road was destroyed and rushed down a steep ravine and across the fords in the river.

There were two aides of General Wilson, Captain Breckinridge and Lieutenant Titus, who were riding in the infantry skirmish line. Captain Paget, the British naval *attaché*, and four correspondents—Millard, Root, Thompson, and myself—were also with them, and we all forded the river together. They had seen General Ernst and his staff a half hour before hurrying toward the town along the Ponce road, and they supposed he had already entered it. Moreover, the road leading into the town was the shortest distance to the place from whence the firing came, so we rode down it at a gallop in order that we might still be in time to see Coamo surrender.

For a mile the road was quite empty, and the houses on either side were either shut and barred or open and deserted. A rifle-pit, also deserted, stretched across the road, but the horses scrambled around it and, turning with the road, brought us into the main street of Coamo. General Ernst was not in the street, nor were there any Spaniards. There was a man with a white flag in the middle of it, and he seemed inclined to drop it and run if needful.

The horses were racing now, and the clatter they made in the empty street was impressive.

Third Wisconsin Volunteers Passing Spanish Rifle-pit Thrown Up Across the Street in Coamo.

Drawn from a photograph taken by the author.

As we passed a few men crawled out from under the porches and shouted, "Vivan los Americanos!" and then ran back again and hid. More men with white flags peeped out from around corners and shook the flags at us frantically.

It was like a horse race, with starters stretched out all along the course. Barricades of iron pipes across the street and more rifle-pits failed to discourage the horses. They were excited by the shouts and by the flags, and they carried us, racing neck and neck, to the other end of Coamo. There we found, to our embarrassment, that it was empty of American troops, and that, unwittingly and unwillingly, we had been offered its surrender.

Captain Breckinridge and Lieutenant Titus looked at each other's shoulder-straps, and Lieutenant Titus congratulated his superior officer on having taken a town of five thousand inhabitants with six men.

Then we borrowed a flag of truce, and with the aid of Captain Paget's red silk handkerchief wigwagged to the Sixteenth that it was perfectly safe to come in.

I took the Spanish flag of the Alcalde, his staff of office, his seals of the city and the key to the cartel. The staff I left with him, the flag I turned over to General Wilson, to whom it, of course, belonged, and the key to the cartel I still retain as a souvenir of the fact that once for twenty minutes, I was mayor and military governor and chief of police of Coamo.

The people were glad to see our troops, but

Main Road Between Ponce and Port Ponce.

there was a difference between the reception they gave them and the reception the people of Ponce gave them, which was as marked as possible. At first the people of Coamo were terrified, and carried brandy bottles with them as being possibly a stronger means of protection than the flags of truce. But as soon as they saw no harm would

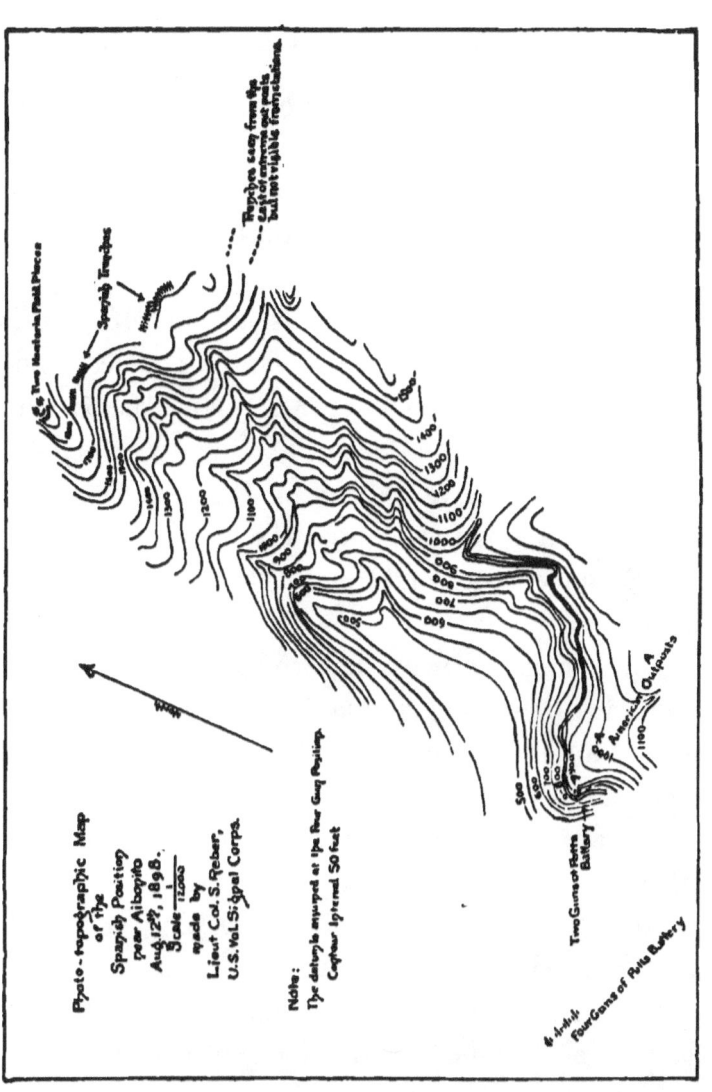

come to them they became more friendly, but not so delirious as were the people of Ponce. The Americans did not care. They sang, "Just tell them that you saw us, and that we were doing well."

General Wilson had established himself in the home of the Alcalde and was sending modest telegrams to the Commander-in-chief at Ponce and receiving congratulations. The men were smoking the cigarettes and drinking the wine the people pressed upon them, and the officers swarmed in the only hotel and fought the skirmish over again.

But someone always has to pay the reckoning, and back of the negro quarter of the town, at the end of an avenue of palms, the men who had paid the heaviest price were being buried in the Catholic graveyard. It was just after sunset, and the place was damp and chilly and dark. Two hospital stewards, who had been keeping count of the Spanish dead as they were put into the graves, sat on a tombstone and checked off the last foreign name on the list with a stub of a pencil.

"Well, that's all," said the hospital steward, as he put on his blouse. "We can go now."

The grave-diggers gathered up their spades and

THE PORTO RICAN CAMPAIGN

looked anxiously for their pay, and the keeper of the graveyard stood at the iron gate and jangled his keys against it as a sign to hurry and that his

Lieut. Browning.   Capt. John C. Groome.   Lieut. McFadden.
Officers of First City Troop of Philadelphia.

supper was waiting. It seemed as though no one had time nor thought to spare for the soldiers who had just been hidden from sight forever. Their Spanish friends in the town had not dared to stand at their graves; their comrades were marching to Coamo as prisoners, or were being driven there wounded in the ambulances. It seemed a pity that there was no priest nor firing-squad nor bugler to sound "Lights out" and to pay the soldiers the last tribute, which is the least tribute a country can pay to the men who die for her. With all the rumors of peace that there were in the air, it seemed a pity that they should have died at all.

The lives of a few Spanish officers would not have counted to the American people, and they probably counted for a great deal to someone somewhere in Spain.

The hospital stewards stood looking at each other doubtfully, as though they were trying to think if there were anything still left to do.

And as they hesitated, there came faintly from the other end of the town the throb and beat of martial music advancing up the main street of Coamo. The old keeper of the graveyard left the gates to lock themselves and hobbled off in pursuit, and from the centre of the town we heard wild shouts of "Viva," and from the negro quarters came the sound of bare feet pattering down the road.

The people of Coamo were turning their backs on the men who had ruled them for a hundred years, and were running to greet their new masters, who had been masters for only the last three hours. The music grew louder and louder and broke into the jubilant swing of a Sousa march.

It was the new step on the floor and the new face at the door. The son and heir was coming fast, blue-shirted, sunburned, girded with glistening cartridges. He was sweeping before him the last traces of a fallen Empire; the sons of the young Republic were tearing down the royal crowns and the double castles over the city halls, opening the iron doors of the city jails and raising the flag of the new Empire over the land of the sugar-cane and the palm.

But the men in the graveyard stopped, and looked back at the fresh earth over the graves and half sheepishly raised their hands in salute, and then walked on toward the town to greet the conquerors.

Three days later General Wilson advanced toward Aibonito and found the Spaniards strongly intrenched with artillery and quick-firing guns upon the high hills which protect that city. An effort to dislodge the enemy was attempted on the day before peace was declared. It was made by the artillery, under Major Lancaster. It advanced to within two thousand yards of the enemy's intrenchments, and unlimbered in a field to the left of the road under a terrific fire of shrapnel, common shell, and Mauser bullets. The Spaniards, fortunately, fired too high to touch the artillery, but did much damage to our infantry on the bluffs above. As a spectacle, it was one of the most picturesque fights of the war. Not only could the artillerymen see each other's guns plainly without the aid of a glass, but they could see the men who served them as well, and they answered shell with shell and with the speed of a ball volleyed across a tennis-net. It was in this fight that a shrapnel-shell struck the road within ten inches of the foot of the British naval *attaché*, Captain Paget, and at the same instant lifted five Wisconsin volunteers off their feet and knocked them down. For a moment, Paget was lost to view in a cloud of dust and smoke, from which no one expected to see him reappear alive, but he strode out of it untouched, remarking, in a tone of extreme annoyance, "There was a shell in the Soudan once did exactly that same thing to me." His tone seemed to suggest that there was a limit to any man's patience. A few minutes later a solitary tree beneath which he was sitting was struck by another shell, which killed two and wounded three men. Major Woodbury, the surgeon-in-chief of the command, who was under fire for the first time, assisted the men to the ambulances, while the Mauser bullets cut many holes in the air above him; he behaved as cheerily as any man I ever saw in a fight. Paget, who had been in a dozen campaigns, took it all as a matter of course, and assisted one of the wounded men out of the range of the bullets from the side of a steep and high hill. The sight did more to popularize the Anglo-American alliance with the soldiers than could the weightiest argument of ambassadors or statesmen.

Just as this fight ended, Lieutenant Hains, whose gun occupied the most exposed position in a turn of the road, and the one farthest in advance, was shot through the body by a bullet. It half turned him, and he staggered into the arms of his sergeant, who caught him around the waist and helped him to the ambulance. One night on the transport, after we had shared a very bad dinner, he had recklessly promised to give me a good one "when we take San Juan," and I had reminded him of this promise frequently. When I came up to him after he was shot, he raised his eyes and said, faintly, "I am afraid I can't give you that dinner at San Juan."

I naturally pretended that I thought he was not badly hurt, and said we would put off the dinner until we met in New York.

"Very well," Hains said, closing his eyes. "If it's just as convenient.to you, we'll wait until we get to New York." A man who can joke about

Battery "A" under Captain Warburton Loading Lighter with Guns.

his dinner engagements when a bullet has just passed through him from his shoulder to his hip is a good man to keep in the army, and fortunately for the army Hains lived.

A day after the fight at Aibonito, Peace laid her detaining hand on the shoulder of each general, and the operations closed for thirty days.

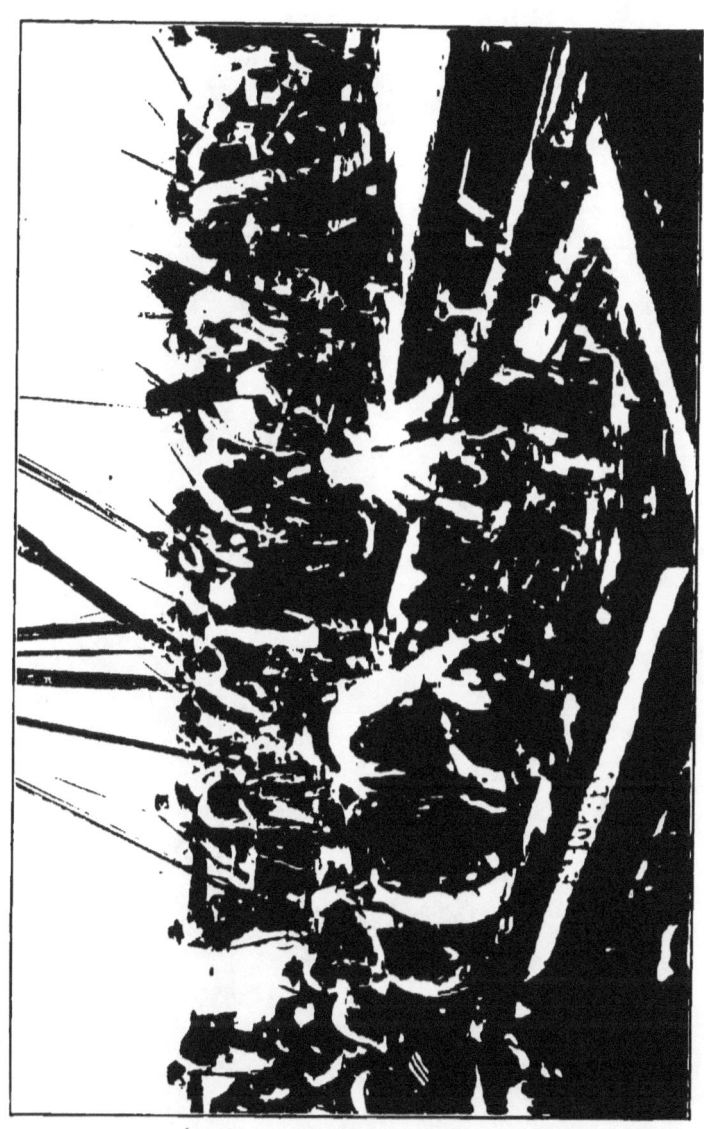

Troops Embarking for Home.

THE PORTO RICAN CAMPAIGN

Peace came differently to different men. One major of volunteers who had already established his nerve on polo-fields and as a most reckless

Sentries at Cavalry Outpost on Cayey Road, about two and a half Miles from Guayana. Established after Protocol.

rider, without a moment's hesitation, threw his hat high in the air and cried, "Thank God! Now I won't get killed." On the other hand, the artillerymen of Battery B of Pennsylvania, when they heard peace had come, swore and hooted and groaned. They were behind a gun pointed at the enemy, who was intrenched to the left of Guayana. The shell was in the chamber, the gunner had aimed the piece and had run backward, but before it spoke, Lieutenant MacLaughlin, of the Signal Corps, galloped upon the scene, shrieking, "Cease firing, peace has been declared!" Whereat the men swore.

Peace came with Porto Rico occupied by our troops and with the Porto Ricans blessing our flags, which must never leave the island. It is a beautiful island, smiling with plenty and content. It will bring us nothing but what is for good, and it came to us willingly with open arms. But had it been otherwise, it would have come to us. The course of empire to-day takes its way to all points of the compass—not only to the West. If it move always as smoothly, as honorably, and as victoriously as it did in Porto Rico, our army and our people need ask for no higher measure of success.

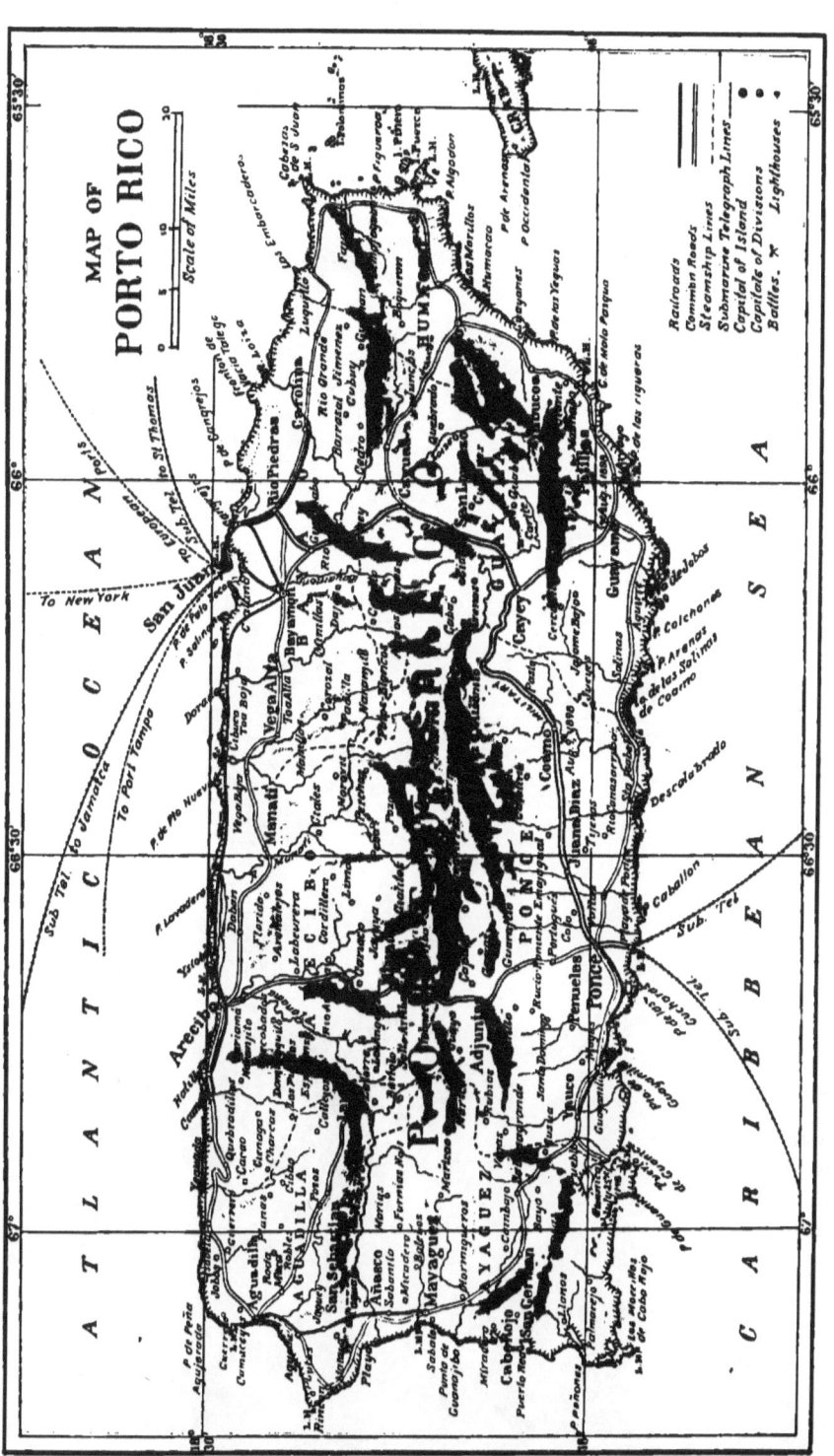

A List of Books by Richard Harding Davis

The Cuban and Porto Rican Campaigns
The King's Jackal   Gallegher, and Other Stories
Soldiers of Fortune   Cinderella, and Other Stories
Stories for Boys

CHARLES SCRIBNER'S SONS, PUBLISHERS

"*Mr. Davis has vigorous ideals—he is in love with strength and cleanness, with 'grit' and resource, with heroism and courage, in men; with beauty and frankness, with freshness and youth, in women; and, liking these qualities, he also likes writing about them. Hence, to those who are of Mr. Davis's mind (as I am for one), Mr. Davis's books are always welcome.*"—The Academy.

THE CUBAN AND PORTO RICAN CAMPAIGNS. With many illustrations from photographs and drawings. Crown 8vo, $1.50.

Mr. Davis's articles in *Scribner's Magazine*, which have given a virtually continuous picture of the war and have attracted a great deal of attention, form the basis for a history of the conflict which Mr. Davis has had in preparation from the beginning. All the vivid and striking passages are retained; but in addition the book has not only the value of a skillful war correspondent's momentary impressions, but of a carefully considered summing-up by an especially competent, serious student of the war.

THE KING'S JACKAL. With illustrations and a cover-design by C. D. Gibson. *Twenty-fifth Thousand.* 12mo, $1.00.

"Mr. Davis has travelled long distances and has seen many strange peoples, and it is therefore scarcely fair to challenge the fidelity of his characters to life, especially in the present instance, where we are introduced into Tangier, and to a circle which includes such a variety of personages as an exiled King of Messina, a disgraced German officer, a retired croupier, a 'fallen angel,' one Prince Kalonay, 'a fellow of the very best blood in Europe and with the very worst morals'; an American correspondent of immense daring, courage, and chivalry; a brilliant woman of easy virtue, and a young California girl with a great fortune, an ardent admiration for brave men, a devotion for the Roman Catholic Church, and an ingenuous character. From such heterogeneous material, it is easy to see that sharp contrasts and surprising complications might result. . . . If we were asked to suggest a story which should keep one for a couple of hours or more in a glow of pleasurable anticipation, by its demands upon our sentiment, we could hardly do better than to name 'The King's Jackal.'"
—Philadelphia *Bulletin.*

SOLDIERS OF FORTUNE. With illustrations and a cover-design by C. D. Gibson. *Fifty-eighth Thousand.* Uniform with "The King's Jackal." 12mo, $1.50.

"Mr. Davis has produced a rousing tale of adventure, with several fine fellows in it, and one woman whom we

are glad to know, and who has gone straight to our hearts and made there for herself a corner that we will keep warm, and to which we will turn with pleasure time and again to love her for all her fine traits—most of all, perhaps, for her genius for *camaraderie*, which found so graceful a climax in the kiss she imprinted on the forehead of the young Englishman who had been murdered by his own treacherous troopers. . . . It is not necessary to commend this story. It has won its way already. But to those who have not yet read it, we can say, ' Do so at once.' "
— *The Critic*.

GALLEGHER, AND OTHER STORIES. With cover-design by A. B. Frost. *Fortieth Thousand.* Uniform with "The King's Jackal" and "Soldiers of Fortune." 12mo, paper, 50 cents; cloth, $1.00.

GALLEGHER
A WALK UP THE AVENUE
MY DISREPUTABLE FRIEND, MR. RAEGEN
THE OTHER WOMAN
THERE WERE NINETY AND NINE
THE TRAILER FOR ROOM NO. 8
THE CYNICAL MISS CATHERWAIGHT
VAN BIBBER AND THE SWAN BOATS
VAN BIBBER'S BURGLAR
VAN BIBBER AS BEST MAN

" Mr. Davis's stories are also of the people and for the people; and their swift, concentrated style makes them grateful reading. Mr. Davis's Fifth Avenue sketches are as unaffected as those of Cherry Street; and while finding them all among the best stories of the year, we confess to a partiality for those which immortalize Van Bibber the dandy, who goes rowing in Central Park with children from the tenement-houses, and lends his aid to elopements and to deserving burglars; never, even under the most trying circumstances, losing the air of wearing an orchid in his buttonhole."—New York *Evening Post*.

CINDERELLA, AND OTHER STORIES. With cover-design by A. B. Wenzell. *Thirteenth Thousand.* Uniform with "The King's Jackal." 12mo, $1.00.

CINDERELLA	AN ASSISTED EMIGRANT
MISS DELAMAR'S UNDERSTUDY	THE REPORTER WHO MADE
THE EDITOR'S STORY	HIMSELF KING

"Mr. Davis's aptitude for work of this kind is too well known to need commendation. There is a freshness and brightness about this volume which is very attractive, for he is one of the writers peculiar to the period, to whom dullness would seem to be impossible. There are five sketches in the book, and each is so good in its way that it is not easy to say which is the best."—*Public Opinion.*

STORIES FOR BOYS. Illustrated, 12mo, $1.00.

"It is a fact, not generally known, but nevertheless a fact, that Richard Harding Davis began his career as a weaver of stories for boys, his first work appearing in *St. Nicholas*. . . . These capital sketches have genuine interest of plot, a hearty, breezy spirit of youth and adventuresomeness which will captivate the special audience they are addressed to and will also charm older people."—Hartford *Courant.*

"All the stories have a verve and fire and movement which is just what boys like."—Boston *Transcript.*

CHARLES SCRIBNER'S SONS
153-157 FIFTH AVENUE   NEW YORK

www.ingramcontent.com/pod-product-compliance
Lightning Source LLC
Chambersburg PA
CBHW030402230426
43664CB00007BB/708